HITLER'S WAR MACHINE

GERMAN TANK HUNTERS
THE PANZERJÄGER

EDITED AND INTRODUCED BY
BOB CARRUTHERS

Pen & Sword
MILITARY

This edition published in 2012 by
Pen & Sword Military
An imprint of
Pen & Sword Books Ltd
47 Church Street
Barnsley
South Yorkshire
S70 2AS

First published in Great Britain in 2012 in digital format by
Coda Books Ltd.

Copyright © Coda Books Ltd, 2012
Published under licence by Pen & Sword Books Ltd.

ISBN 978 1 78159 132 1

Printed and bound by CPI Group (UK) Ltd, Croydon, CR0 4YY

Pen & Sword Books Ltd incorporates the Imprints of Pen & Sword Aviation, Pen &
Sword Family History, Pen & Sword Maritime, Pen & Sword Military, Pen &
Sword Discovery, Pen & Sword Politics, Pen & Sword Atlas, Pen & Sword
Archaeology, Wharncliffe Local History, Wharncliffe True Crime, Wharncliffe
Transport, Pen & Sword Select, Pen & Sword Military Classics, Leo Cooper, The
Praetorian Press, Claymore Press, Remember When, Seaforth Publishing and
Frontline Publishing

For a complete list of Pen & Sword titles please contact
PEN & SWORD BOOKS LIMITED
47 Church Street, Barnsley, South Yorkshire, S70 2AS, England
E-mail: enquiries@pen-and-sword.co.uk
Website: www.pen-and-sword.co.uk

CONTENTS

INTRODUCTION

This book forms part of the series entitled 'Hitler's War Machine.' The aim is to provide the reader with a varied range of materials drawn from original writings covering the strategic, operational and tactical aspects of the weapons and battles of Hitler's war. The concept behind the series is to provide the well-read and knowledgeable reader with an interesting compilation of related primary sources combined with the best of what is in the public domain to build a picture of a particular aspect of that titanic struggle.

I am pleased to report that the series has been well received and it is a pleasure to be able to bring original primary sources to the attention of an interested readership. I particularly enjoy discovering new primary sources, and I am pleased to be able to present them unadorned and unvarnished to a sophisticated audience. The primary sources such as Die Wehrmacht and Signal, speak for themselves and the readership I strive to serve is the increasingly well informed community of reader/historians which needs no editorial lead and can draw its own conclusions. I am well aware that our community is constantly striving to discover new nuggets of information, and I trust that with this volume I have managed to stimulate fresh enthusiasm and that at least some of these facts and articles will be new to you and will provoke readers to research further down these lines of investigation, and perhaps cause established views to be challenged once more. I am aware at all times in compiling these materials that our relentless pursuit of more and better historical information is at the core our common passion. I trust that this selection will contribute to that search and will help all of us to better comprehend and understand the bewildering events of the last century.

In order to produce an interesting compilation giving a flavour of events at the tactical and operational level I have returned once more to the wartime US Intelligence series of pamphlets, which contain an intriguing series of contemporary articles on weapons and tactics. I find this series of pamphlets particularly fascinating as they are written in, what was then, the present tense and therefore provide us with a sense of what was happening at the face of battle as events unfolded.

Thank you for buying this volume in the series we hope you will enjoy discovering some new insights you will go on to try the others in the series.

Bob Carruthers
Edinburgh 2012

GERMAN TANK HUNTERS

The first weapon of the German Panzerjäger (armour hunters or tank hunters) was the humble Panzerbüchse which was in service from 1917 through to 1943. Panzerbüchse literally means "armour rifle" and German anti-tank rifles originated back in 1917 with the Mauser 1918 T-Gewehr, the world's first anti-tank rifle. It was created as an immediate response to the appearance of British tanks on the Western Front. A single shot manually operated rifle, it enjoyed moderate success, with approximately 15,800 rifles eventually produced. The Panzerbüchse 39 (PzB 39) was the main German anti-tank rifle used in World War II. It was an improvement of the unsuccessful Panzerbüchse 38 (PzB 38) rifle.

German Panzerbüchse development resumed in the late 1930s. In an effort to provide infantry with a man-portable lightweight anti-tank rifle. The task fell to Dipl.-Ing. (certified engineer) B. Brauer at Gustloff Werke in Suhl who designed the Panzerbüchse 38 (PzB 38). It was a manually loaded single-shot weapon with a recoiling barrel. When fired, the barrel recoiled about 9 cm, which opened the breech and ejected the spent cartridge casing. The breech block was then arrested in the rear position, remaining opened for the gunner to manually insert a new cartridge. The gunner then released the cocked breech with a lever at the grip. The breech and barrel would then move forward again and the trigger was cocked in preparation to fire. This rather complicated mechanism was prone to jamming as the system easily fouled in field use.

Although manufactured with pressed steel parts that were spot-welded, because of the complicated vertical breech block mechanism the Panzerbüchse 38 was difficult to manufacture and only a small number of 1,408 PzB 38 rifles were built in

1939 and 1940 at the Gustloff Werke plant; only 62 of these weapons were used by German troops in the invasion of Poland in 1939.

The Panzerbüchse 39 was the next development, and was found to be a major improvement as a result the Panzerbüchse 38 declared obscelescent and production was immediately switched to the Panzerbüchse 39. However it too featured a vertical breech block mechanism and used the same cartridge. It retained the barrel of the PzB 38 and had an only slightly increased overall length of 162.0 centimetres (63.8 in); weight was reduced to 12.6 kilograms (28 lb). Its performance data was basically the same as that of the PzB 38. To increase the practical rate of fire, two cartridge-holding cases containing 10 rounds each could be attached to both sides of the weapon near the breech - these were not magazines feeding the weapon, they simply enabled the loader to extract the cartridges (that he still had to manually insert into the gun) from the conveniently placed magazines. 568 PzB 39 were used by the German army in the invasion of Poland; two years later, at the beginning of the war against Russia, 25,298 PzB 39 were in use by German troops; total production from March 1940 to November 1941, when production ceased, was 39,232 rifles. The PzB 39 remained in use until 1944, by which time it had become hopelessly inadequate against all but the lightest armored vehicles.

OKW recognised the need for a more powerful form of anti-tank weapon and the design of a horse-drawn, 3.7 cm anti-tank gun (designated 3.7 cm Pak L/45) by Rheinmetall commenced in 1924 and the first guns were issued in 1928. However, by the early 1930s, it was apparent that horse-drawn artillery was obsolescent, and the gun was modified for motorized transport by substituting magnesium-alloy wheels with pneumatic tyres for the original spoked wooden wheels. Re-designated the 3.7 cm Pak 35/36, it began to replace the 3.7 Pak L/45 in 1934 and first appeared in combat in 1936 during the Spanish Civil War. It formed the basis for many other nations' anti-tank guns during the first years of World War II. The KwK 36 L/45 was the same gun but adapted as the main armament on several tanks, most notably the early models of the Panzer III.

The Pak 36, being a small-calibre weapon, was outdated by the May 1940 Western Campaign, and crews found them inadequate against allied tanks like the British Mk.II Matilda, and the French Char B1 and Somua S35. Still, the gun was effective against the most common light tanks, such as the Renault FT-17 and saw wide service during the Battle of France and the T-26 during Operation Barbarossa. The widespread introduction of medium tanks quickly erased the gun's effectiveness; miserable performance against the T-34 on the Eastern Front led to the Pak 36 being derisively dubbed the "Door Knocker" (Heeresanklopfgerät, literally "army door-knocking device") for its inability to do anything other than advertise its presence to a T-34 by futilely bouncing rounds off its armor.

Not surprisingly the Pak 36 began to be replaced by the new 5 cm Pak 38 in mid 1940. The addition of tungsten-core shells (Pzgr. 40) added slightly to the armour penetration of the Pak 36. Despite its continued impotence against the T-34, it remained the standard anti-tank weapon for many units until 1942. It was discovered that Pak 36 crews could still achieve kills on T-34s, but this rare feat required tungsten-cored armour piercing ammunition and a direct shot to the rear or side armour from point-blank range.

As the Pak 36 was gradually replaced, many were removed from their carriages and added to SdKfz 251 halftracks to be used as light anti-armour support. The guns were also passed on to the forces of Germany's allies fighting on the Eastern Front, such as the 3rd and 4th Romanian Army. This proved particularly disastrous during the Soviet encirclement (Operation Uranus) at the Battle of Stalingrad when these Romanian forces were targeted to bear the main Soviet armoured thrust. The Pak 36 also served with the armies of Finland (notably during the defence of Suomussalmi), it was also deployed in Hungary, and Slovakia.

In 1943, the introduction of the Stielgranate 41 shaped charge meant that the Pak 36 could now penetrate any armour, although the low velocity of the projectile limited its range. The Pak 36s, together with the new shaped charges, were issued to Fallschirmjäger units and other light troops. The gun's light weight meant that it could be easily moved by hand, and this mobility made it ideal for their purpose.

The replacement for the outdated Pak 36 was the 50cm Pak 38. The longer barrel and larger projectile produced the required level of kinetic energy to pierce armour . The PaK 38 was first used by the German forces during the Second World War in April 1941. When the Germans faced Soviet tanks in 1941 during Operation Barbarossa, the PaK 38 was one of the few early guns capable of effectively penetrating the 45 mm (1.8 in) armor of the formidable T-34. Additionally, the gun was also equipped with Panzergranate 40 APCR projectiles which had a hard tungsten core, in an attempt to penetrate the armor of the heavier KV-1 tank. Although it was soon replaced by more powerful weapons, the Pak 38 remained a potent and useful weapon and remained in service with the Wehrmacht until the end of the war.

The 7.5 cm PaK 40 (7.5 cm Panzerabwehrkanone 40) was the next generation of anti-tank gun to see service. This German 7.5 centimetre high velocity anti-tank gun was developed in 1939-1941 by Rheinmetall and used extensively from 1942-1945 during the Second World War. It was the PaK 40 which formed the backbone of German anti-tank guns for the latter part of World War II. Development of the PaK 40 began in 1939 with development contracts being placed with Krupp and Rheinmetall to develop a 7.5 cm anti-tank gun. Priority of the project was

A half-track of the Grossdeutschland Division equipped with a 2.8 KWK anti-tank gun, Russia 1941.

initially low, but Operation Barbarossa in 1941 and the sudden appearance of heavily armoured Soviet tanks like the T-34 and KV-1, increased the priority. The first pre-production guns were delivered in November 1941.

In April 1942, Wehrmacht had 44 guns in service. It was remarkably successful weapon and by 1943 the PaK 40 formed the bulk of the German anti-tank artillery.The PaK 40 was the standard German anti-tank gun until the end of the war, and was supplied by Germany to its allies. Some captured guns were used by the Red Army. After the end of the war the PaK 40 remained in service in several European armies, including Albania, Bulgaria, Czechoslovakia, Finland, Norway, Hungary and Romania.

Around 23,500 PaK 40 werc produced, and about 6,000 more were used to arm tank destroyers. The unit manufacturing cost amounted to 2200 man-hours at a cost of 12000 RM. A lighter automatic version, the heaviest of the Bordkanone series of heavy calibre aircraft ordnance as the BK 7,5 was used in the Henschel Hs129 aircraft.

The Pak 40 was effective against almost every Allied tank

until the end of the war. However, the PaK 40 was much heavier than the 50 cm PaK 38, It was difficult to manhandle into position and its mobility was limited. It was difficult or impossible to move without an artillery tractor on boggy ground.

The PaK 40 debuted in Russia where it was needed to combat the newest Soviet tanks there. It was designed to fire the same low-capacity APCBC, HE and HL projectiles which had been standardized for usage in the long barreled Kampfwagenkanone KwK 40 main battle tank-mounted guns. In addition there was an APCR shot for the PaK 40, a munition which eventually became very scarce.

The main differences amongst the rounds fired by 75 mm German guns were in the length and shape of the cartridge cases for the PaK 40. The 7.5 cm KwK (tank) fixed cartridge case is twice the length of the 7.5 cm KwK 37 (short barrelled 75 mm), and the 7.5 cm PaK 40 cartridge is a third longer than the 7.5 cm KwK 40.

The longer cartridge case allowed a larger charge to be used and a higher velocity for the Armour Piercing Capped Ballistic Cap round to be achieved. The muzzle velocity was about 790 m/s (2,600 ft/s) as opposed to 750 m/s (2,500 ft/s) for the KwK 40 L/43. This velocity was available for about one year after the weapon's introduction. Around the same time, the Panzer IVs 7.5 cm KwK 40 L/43 gun and the nearly identical Sturmkanone (StuK) 40 L/43 began to be upgraded with barrels that were 48 calibers long, or L/48, which remained the standard for them until the end of the war.

In the field, an alarming number of L/48 cartridge cases carrying the hotter charge failed to be ejected properly from the weapon's semi-automatic breech, even on the first shot (in vehicles).[citation needed] Rather than re-engineer the case, German Ordnance reduced the charge loading until the problem went away. The new charge brought the muzzle velocity down to 750 m/s, or about 10 m/s higher than the original L/43 version of the weapon. Considering the average variability in large round velocities from a given gun, this is virtually negligible in effect. The first formal documentation of this decision appears on May 15, 1943 ("7.5cm Sturmkanone 40 Beschreibung") which details a side by side comparison of the L/43 and the L/48 weapons. The synopsis provided indicates very little difference in the guns, meaning the upgrade had little if any benefit.

All further official presentations of the KwK 40 L/48 ("Oberkommando des Heeres, Durchschlagsleistungen panzerbrechender Waffen") indicate a muzzle velocity of 750 m/s for the gun. As for the PaK 40, the desire for commonality again appears to have prevailed since the APCBC charge was reduced to 750 m/s, even though case ejection failures apparently were never a problem in the PaK version of the gun.

For reasons which seem to be lost to history, at least some 75 mm APCBC cartridges appear to have received a charge which produced a muzzle velocity of about 770 m/s (2,500 ft/s). The first documented firing by the U.S. of a PaK 40 recorded an average muzzle velocity of 776 m/s for its nine most instrumented firings. Probably because of these results, period intelligence publications ("Handbook on German Military Forces") gave 770 m/s as the PaK 40 APCBC muzzle velocity, although post war pubs corrected this (Department of the Army Pamphlet No. 30-4-4, "Foreign Military Weapons and Equipment (U) Vol. 1 Artillery (U) dated August of 1955-this document was originally classified).

In addition, German sources are contradictory in that the Official Firing Table document for the 75 mm KwK 40, StuK 40, and the PaK 40 dated October, 1943 cites 770 m/s on one of the APCBC tables therein, showing some confusion. ("Schusstafel fur die 7.5cm Kampfwagenkanone 40").

The 88 mm gun (eighty-eight) was a German anti-aircraft and anti-tank artillery gun from World War II. It was widely used by Germany throughout the war, and was one of the most recognized German weapons of the war. Development of the original models led to a wide variety of guns.

The name applies to a series of guns, the first one officially called the 8,8 cm Flak 18, the improved 8,8 cm Flak 36, and later the 8,8 cm Flak 37. Flak is a contraction of German Flugzeugabwehrkanone meaning "anti-aircraft cannon", the original purpose of the eighty-eight. In informal German use, the guns were universally known as the Acht-acht ("eight-eight"), a contraction of Acht-komma-acht Zentimeter ("8.8 cm"). In English, "flak" became a generic term for ground anti-aircraft fire.

The versatile carriage allowed the eighty-eight to be fired in a limited anti-tank mode when still on wheels, and to be completely emplaced in only two-and-a-half minutes. Its successful use as an improvised anti-tank gun led to the development of a tank gun based upon it. These related guns served as the main armament of tanks such as the Tiger I: the 8.8 cm KwK 36, with the "KwK" abbreviation standing for KampfwagenKanone ("fighting vehicle cannon").

In addition to these Krupp's designs, Rheinmetall created later a more powerful anti-aircraft gun, the 8,8 cm Flak 41, produced in relatively small numbers. Krupp responded with another prototype of the long-barreled 88 mm gun, which was further developed into the anti-tank and tank destroyer 8.8 cm Pak 43 gun, and turret-mounted 8.8 cm KwK 43 heavy tank gun.

BACKGROUND

Initially anti-aircraft artillery guns of World War I were adaptations of existing medium-calibre weapons mounted to allow fire at higher angles. By 1915 the German command realized that these are useless for anything beyond deterrence, even against the vulnerable balloons and slow-moving aircraft. With the increase of aircraft performance, many armies developed dedicated AA guns with high muzzle velocity – allowing the projectiles to reach greater altitudes – and high rate of fire. The first such German gun was introduced in 1917, and it used calibre 88 mm, common in the German navy.

After losing the war, Germany had been forbidden to procure new weapons of most types. Nevertheless, the Krupp company started the development of a new gun in partnership with Bofors of Sweden. The original design was a 75 mm model. During the prototype phase, the army asked for a gun with considerably greater capability. The designers started over using 88 mm caliber.

Prototype 88s were first produced in 1928. These early models, the Flak 18, used a single-piece barrel with a length of 56 calibres, leading to the commonly-seen designation L/56.

The Flak 18 was mounted on a cruciform gun carriage. A simple to operate "semi-automatic" loading system ejected fired shells, allowing it to be reloaded by simply inserting a new shell into a tray. The gun would then fire, recoil, and, during the return stroke, the empty casing would be thrown backward by levers, and a cam would engage and recock the gun. This resulted in firing rates of 15 to 20 rounds a minute, which was better than similar weapons of the era. High explosive ammunition was used against aircraft and personnel, and armour-piercing and high-explosive anti-tank against tanks and other armoured vehicles.

Widespread production started with the Nazi rise to power in 1933, and the Flak 18 was available in small numbers when Germany intervened in the Spanish Civil War. It quickly proved to be the best anti-aircraft weapon then available. Further, the high muzzle velocity and large calibre made it an excellent long-range anti-vehicle weapon. This experience also demonstrated a number of minor problems and potential improvement opportunities.

Many of these were incorporated into the Flak 36, which had a two-piece barrel for easier replacement of worn liners. The new, heavier, carriage allowed it to fire while in an emergency mode when still on wheels and without grounding outriggers, but with a very limited traverse and elevation. For normal emplacement, one single-axle bogie was detached from the front outrigger, one from the rear outrigger, and side outriggers were hinged from vertical position to the ground, which was estimated at a minimum of two-and-a-half minutes.Both modes of operation made the gun much more suitable for fast-moving operations, the basic concept of the blitzkrieg. Flak 36s were often fitted with an armoured shield that provided limited protection for the gunners. The weight of the gun meant that only large vehicles could move it, and the SdKfz 7 half-track became a common prime mover.

Targeting indicators were attached from the central controller to each of the four guns of a battery, allowing for coordinated fire. Indeed, with the automatic loading system, the gun layers' job was to keep the gun barrel trained on the target area based on the signals from the controller. The loaders would keep the Flak fed with live ammunition which would fire immediately upon insertion—all while the gun layer aimed the weapon according to the data.

The later Flak 37 included updated instrumentation to allow the gun layers to follow directions from the single director more easily. The parts of the various versions of the guns were

North Africa, towed behind an SdKfz 7. Side outriggers lifted for transport visible right behind the gun shield.

interchangeable, and it was not uncommon for various parts to be "mixed and matched" on a particular example. Some sources mistakenly cite that the Flak 37 was not equipped for anti-armour purposes. The fact is all 8.8 cm Flaks were capable of the dual role.

Due to the problems of defending against attack by high-flying aircraft the Luftwaffe asked for newer weapons with even better performance as early as 1939. Rheinmetall responded with a new 88 mm L/71 design with a longer cartridge, the 8,8 cm Flak 41, with a prototype ready in 1941. It fired a 9.4-kilogram (20 lb) shell at a muzzle velocity of 1000 m/s (3,280 ft/s), giving it an effective ceiling of 11,300 meters (37,100 ft) and a maximum of 15,000 meters (49,000 ft), which General Otto Wilhelm von Renz said to be "almost equal to the 128-mm." It featured a lower silhouette on its turntable mounting than did the 8.8-cm Flak 18/36/37 on its pedestal mounting. Two types of gun barrel were used, with three or four sections. Improvements in reloading raised the firing rate, with 20 to 25 rounds a minute being quoted.

The first 44 guns produced (August 1942) were immediately sent to Tunisia but, because of problems in service, the guns were afterwards used mostly in Germany where they could be properly maintained and serviced. The Flak 41 had the disadvantage of complexity, and was prone to problems with ammunition, cases often jamming on extraction. Because of the high cost and complexity of this Flak gun, the Germans manufactured relatively few of them, 556 in all. As of August 1944 only 157 were fielded, and 318 in January 1945. A final adaptation, known as the Flak 37/41, mounted the Flak 41 gun on the Flak 37 carriage, but only 13 were produced.

Production numbers

Thousands of 88 mm guns were produced throughout the war in various models and mounts.

Heavy flak production numbers	pre-war	1939	1940	1941	1942	1943	1944	1945	Total
8.8 cm Flak 18/36/37	2,459	183	1,130	1,998	3,052	4,712	6,482	738	20,754
8.8 cm Flak 41	0	0	0	0	48	122	290	96?	556
10.5 cm Flak 38/39	?	38	290	509	701	1,220	1,331	92	more than 4,181
12.8 cm Flak 40 (including twins)	0	0	0	0	65	298	664	98	1,125

Comparing to other artillery types, in December 1943, German industry made for example 570 heavy (caliber 88–128 mm) flak guns, 1020 field artillery pieces (caliber 75–210 mm), and 1300 tank guns, anti-tank guns, plus self-propelled guns.

COMBAT HISTORY

The eighty-eight was used in two roles: as a mobile heavy anti-aircraft gun, and in a more static role for home defence.

Anti-aircraft defense of the Reich

From 1935 onwards, the anti-aircraft defense of Nazi Germany was controlled by the Luftwaffe. By 1 September 1939, at the beginning of World War II, the Luftwaffe anti-aircraft artillery employed 6,700 light (2 cm and 3,7 cm) flak guns and 2,628 heavy flak guns. Of the latter, a small number were 10.5 cm Flak 38 or 39 and the majority were 8.8 cm Flak 18, 36 or 37. This was twice as many heavy flak guns as Air Defence of Great Britain (ADGB) had at the time, with France and the United States having even less.

Throughout the entire war, the majority of the 88 mm guns were used in their original anti-aircraft role.

The pecuniary costs associated with anti-aircraft cannon were substantial, especially when compared to fighter aircraft. For example, in January 1943 – at a time Germany was desperately fighting to regain strategic initiative in the East and also faced a heavy bombing campaign in the West – expenditures on flak were 39 million reichsmark, whereas all the remaining weapon production and munitions production amounted to 93 million (including 20 million of the navy budget and only 9 million of aircraft-related budget).

By August 1944, there were 10,704 Flak 18, 36 and 37 guns in service, now complemented also by the formidable 12.8 cm Flak 40, owing to the increase in U.S. and British bombing raids during 1943 and 1944. There were complaints that, due to the apparent ineffectiveness of anti-aircraft defenses as a whole, the

In combat, USSR, 1942

guns should be transferred from air defense units to anti-tank duties, but this politically unpopular move was never made.

Support of German ground troops

The 88 performed well in its original role of an anti-aircraft gun, but it proved to be a superb anti-tank gun as well. Its success was due to its versatility: the standard anti-aircraft platform allowed gunners to depress the muzzle below horizontal, unlike most other anti-aircraft guns. During the initial stages of the war, as it was becoming increasingly clear that existing anti-tank weapons were unable to pierce the armour of heavier enemy tanks, gunners increasingly put the weapon to use against enemy tanks, a situation that was aided by the prevalence of the 88 among German forces.

Similarly to the anti-aircraft role, in the anti-tank role the 88 guns were tactically arranged into batteries, usually four guns each. The higher-level tactical unit was, most commonly, a mixed anti-aircraft battalion (Flak-Abteilung, gemischte). It totaled 12 such guns on average, supplanted by light cannons.

The German Condor Legion made extensive use of the 88 in

the Spanish Civil War, where its usefulness as an anti-tank weapon and a general artillery piece exceeded its role as an anti-aircraft weapon.

For the 1940 Battle of France, the army was supported by eighty-eights deployed in twenty-four mixed flak battalions. The eighty-eight was used against heavily armored tanks such as the Char B1 bis and Matilda II, whose frontal armour could not be penetrated by the light 3.7 cm anti-tank guns then available. The 88 was powerful enough to penetrate over 84 mm of armour at a range of 2 km, making it an unparalleled anti-tank weapon during the early war, and still formidable against all but the heaviest tanks at the end of the war. Notably, Erwin Rommel's timely use of the gun to blunt the British counterattack at Arras ended any hope of a breakout from the blitzkrieg encirclement of May 1940. In the entire Battle of France, flak destroyed 152 tanks and 151 bunkers.

During the North African campaign, Rommel made the most effective use of the weapon, as he lured tanks of the British 8th Army into traps by baiting them with apparently retreating tanks. When the enemy tanks pursued, concealed 88s picked them off at ranges far beyond those of their 2-pdr and 6-pdr guns. A mere two flak battalions destroyed 264 tanks throughout 1941.

For the invasion of the Soviet Union Germany deployed the 88s in 51 mixed flak battalions. They were mostly Luftwaffe-subordinated units attached to the Heer on a corps or army level, with approximately one battalion per corps. The weapon saw continuous use on the eastern front. The appearance of the outstanding T-34 and KV tanks shocked the German tank crews and antitank teams, who could only penetrate the Soviet tanks' armour at extremely close range when using the standard 37 mm and 50 mm guns.

The 88 was arguably most effective in the flat and open terrain of Libya, Egypt and the eastern front. The less open terrain in Italy and Northern France was less suitable for the 88.

Manhandling

The success of the 88 caused the Allies to take steps to defend against it in new tank designs.

By February 1945, there were 327 heavy anti-aircraft batteries delegated against the Soviet land armies, which was 21% of those dedicated solely to anti-aircraft defense of the country.

Use by other armed forces

The Flak 36 guns were briefly issued in late 1944 to the American 7th Army as captured weapons. The 79th Field Artillery Battalion (Provisional) was formed from personnel of the 79th and 179th Field Artillery Groups to fire captured German artillery pieces at the height of an ammunition shortage. Similarly, the 244th Field Artillery Battalion was temporarily equipped with a miscellany of captured German 88mm guns and 105mm and 150mm howitzers.

The Flak 18 was not as powerful as its Italian or Allied counterparts. As an anti-aircraft gun it fired a 9.2 kilogram (20 lb) shell at a muzzle velocity of 790 m/s (2,600 ft/s) to an effective ceiling of 7,900 meters (25,900 ft) (at maximum 10,600 meters (34,800 ft)). Although this was useful against U.S. daylight raids, which typically flew at 7,600 meters (24,900 ft), many aircraft could fly higher than its maximum effective ceiling. In comparison, the British 3.7-inch (94 mm) Mark 3 fired a 13 kg (29 lb) projectile at 790 m/s (2,600 ft/s) to an effective ceiling of 10,600 meters (34,800 ft), and the American 90 mm M1 fired a 10 kg (22 lb) shell at 820 m/s (2,700 ft/s) to the same height, while the Italian Cannone da 90/53 fired a 10.33 kg projectile at 830 m/s to an effective ceiling of 12,000 meters (39,000 ft). The Allied weapons' capabilities were augmented by the introduction of proximity fuses, which allowed them to remain effective even with the introduction of jet-engined aircraft. The Allies' and Italian weapons were heavier and less mobile, with the Allied weapons being almost useless for ground fire until numerous modifications were carried out. While the U.S. and Italian 90 mm would go on to serve as powerful anti-tank guns, they were by no means as widely deployed as tank-killers as was the German 88.

Pak 43 and KwK 43

At the time Rheinmetall developed Flak 41, Krupp's tried to compete with their 8.8 cm Gerät 42 proposal, but it was not accepted for production as an anti-aircraft gun. Krupp continued development, resulting in the dreaded 8.8 cm Pak 43 anti-tank gun and 8.8 cm KwK 43 tank gun.

Pak 43 (abbreviation of Panzerabwehrkanone 43) used a new cruciform mount with the gun much closer to the ground, making it far easier to hide and harder to hit. It was also provided with a much stronger and more angled armour shield to provide better protection. All versions were able to penetrate about 200 mm of armour at 1,000 m, allowing it to defeat the armor of any contemporary tank. The standard armament of the Tiger II, the KwK 43 tank gun, was essentially the Pak 43 externally modified to fit into a turret. There were also self-propelled versions of the gun, including the lightly-armored Nashorn and, later, strongly-armored Jagdpanther tank destroyers.

German 88 mm anti-aircraft gun display at Land Warfare Hall, Imperial War Museum, Duxford

THE 88 'FAMILY'

Guns using the early 88×571R mm cartridge

8.8 cm Flak 18: New semi-automatic breech, high velocity gun. Entered production in Germany in 1933. Used the Sonderanhänger 201 trailer. Weight 7 tonnes. Rate of fire 15 to 20 rounds per minute. Later, fitted with a gun shield to protect the crew when engaging ground targets. Produced by Krupp.

> **Mod 1938 II:** Approximately 50 guns modified so a single man could adjust elevation and traverse.

8.8 cm Flak 36: Entered service 1936–37. It used the redesigned trailer Sonderanhänger 202 enabling faster time to action from the move. The SdAnh 202 had twin wheels on two similar carriages. Could engage ground targets from its traveling position. Weight 7 tonnes. Rate of fire 15 to 20 rounds per minute. Produced by Krupp. Later, fitted with a shield to protect the crew when engaging ground targets.

8.8 cm KwK 36: Main gun of the PzKw VI Ausf. E (Tiger I) tank. Despite its designation, some classify it as a parallel development with very similar specifications rather than a derivative of the Flak 36.

8.8 cm Flak 37: An updated version of the Flak 36, the main difference being Übertragungser 37 (a data transmission system). Produced by Krupp.

Guns using the 88×855R mm cartridge

8.8 cm Flak 41: A gun developed and produced by Rheinmetall-Borsig. A 71 caliber barrel and a 855 mm cartridge case. Fitted to the existing Sonderanhänger 202 as standard. Entered service 1943.

8.8 cm Gerät 42: a new Krupp design to compete with Flak 41; did not enter service as an anti-aircraft gun. Further development of the weapon led to the Pak 43 anti-tank gun.

8.8 cm Pak 43: Anti-tank model developed from Krupp's 8.8 cm Gerät 42. New gun carriage, the Sonderanhänger 204. Developed by Krupp and manufactured in different versions, including KwK 43, by at least Dortmund Hoerder-Hüttenverein, Henschel, Weserhütte and Fr. Garny. A 71 caliber barrel and a 822 mm cartridge case.

GERMAN BALANCED ANTITANK PROTECTION

From Tactical and Technical Trends
No. 5, August 13th, 1942

The German 88-mm. dual-purpose AA and AT gun has been a vital factor in Rommel's African campaigns. However, this gun is only one element in the excellent antitank organization of the Germans and should be viewed in its proper perspective.

In accordance with German Army principles, each combat unit, from the smallest to the largest, is so organized, armed, and equipped as to be tactically self-sufficient. Antitank protection is vital to the successful accomplishment of a combat mission; therefore, suitable antitank weapons are provided for each unit. These weapons are used in accordance with the German doctrine of antitank defense, which may be summarized as follows:

Staffs, troops, and supply echelons must be prepared for a tank attack at all times. Careful ground and air reconnaissance and map study assist in indicating the avenues of approach feasible for hostile tank attacks. Certain terrain features are natural obstacles to tanks and must be used to full advantage. The favorable avenues of approach must be protected by antitank guns, artillery, mines, and tanks.

The antitank units, organically a part of infantry regiments, battalions, or companies contribute their fire power to the support and protection of their respective organizations. Those antitank units which are organically a part of corps and divisions, constitute a reserve force which, because of their mobility, can be rushed to decisive areas as determined by the general situation.

Early information relative to hostile tanks permits timely and coordinated defensive measures. All reconnaissance agencies must be required to report immediately tank information to the commander and to the troops specifically threatened.

Certain situations may require the attachment of additional units to antitank battalions such as signal, engineer, and infantry troops.

Antitank protection has been provided for in each of the units, from the smallest to the largest; furthermore, the amount of protection is being steadily increased.

Each infantry company is protected by a section of 3 AT rifles. In Africa, each company of a light division was reported to be equipped with two 76.2-mm. captured Russian field guns for antitank use. (However, see this publication, No. 3, p. 5). Each infantry battalion is protected by 9 AT rifles.

Each regiment is protected by 27 AT rifles and by an AT company which has 3 platoons, each armed with four 37-mm. AT guns (total 12), and one platoon of four 20-mm. rapid fire AA-AT guns.

A trend toward substitution of the 50-mm. AT gun for the 37-mm. AT gun is progressing rapidly.

The infantry division is protected by 81 AT rifles, forty-eight 20-mm. AA-AT guns, and seventy-five 37-mm. or 50-mm. AT guns. The divisional AT battalion has 3 companies of twelve 37-mm. AT guns each and one company of twelve 20-mm. AA-AT guns. One AA battalion of twenty-four 20-mm. AA-AT guns and nine 37-mm. AA guns, or of thirty-six 20-mm. AA-AT guns may be attached.

The motorized division is protected by fifty-four AT rifles, twelve 20-mm AA-AT guns, fifty-four 37-mm. AT guns, and nine 50-mm. AT guns. The motorized AT battalion has 3 companies of eight 37-mm. and three 50-mm. AT guns and one company of twelve 37-mm. AA-AT guns. An AA battalion of twenty-four 20-mm. AA-AT guns and nine 37-mm. AA guns may be attached.

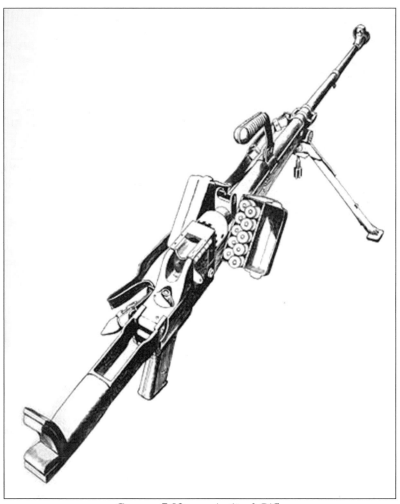

German 7.92-mm. Antitank Rifle

The armored division is protected by high velocity guns mounted in the tanks (totaling one hundred seventeen 37-mm. or 50-mm. high velocity guns), by an AT battalion with twelve 37-mm. and eighteen 50-mm. AT guns, or an AT battalion with twenty-four 47-mm. self-propelled AT guns each mounted on a Mark I tank chassis with a three-sided armor shield, and by an AA Battalion with thirty-three 20-mm. guns.

A mobile AA battalion from the air force is often attached to a division when additional protection is required. This battalion contains 3 heavy batteries of 88-mm. AA guns, each battery consisting of four 88-mm. AA guns and two 20-mm. AA guns; 2 light batteries, each consisting of fifteen 20-mm. AA-AT guns and four 60-cm. searchlights; 1 searchlight battery consisting of nine 150-cm. searchlights and 6 sound locators.

Generally speaking, antitank weapons are of two types: either single-purpose, such as the 50-mm. AT gun, or dual-purpose, such as the highly effective 88-mm. AT and AA gun. The characteristics of the most commonly employed AT weapons may be summarized as follows:

I. SINGLE-PURPOSE ANTITANK WEAPONS

7.92-mm. AT Rifle (See sketch)

Specifications:

- Weight: 27 1/4 lbs.
- Length (shoulder rest extended): 62 1/4 in.
- Length (shoulder rest folded): 50 3/8 in.
- Rate of Fire: 6-8 r.p.m.
- Muzzle velocity: 3,540 f.s.
- Penetration (Homo hard armor-plate at 100 yds., 90°): 33 mm. (1.3 in.)

Remarks: This AT rifle has a hand-lever-operated dropping block and is a single loader. Its ammunition is a special high-velocity armor-piercing type with a super-heavy charge contained in a 13.2-mm. case necked down to take a 7.92-mm. tungsten-carbide cored bullet.

37-mm. AT Gun

Specifications:

- Maximum range: 4,400 yds.
- Penetration (steel plate at 90°): 43 mm. (1.7 in.) at 330 yds., 33 mm. (1.3 in.) at 650 yds.
- Rate of fire: 12 r.p.m.
- Traverse (trails closed): 4°
- Traverse (trails open): 58°

- Weight of AP shell: 1.68 lbs.
- Weight of HE shell: 1.37 lbs.

Remarks: This is one of the main antitank weapons. The gun has two shields, fitted one above the other. The upper shield moves with the gun in traverse. There are four types of shell: armor-piercing with and without tracer, and high explosive with and without tracer. The gun is mounted on a well-sprung carriage and is fitted with low-pressure pneumatic tires for transportation as a motor trailer. It can be drawn by a detachment of soldiers across country for short distances.

47-mm. AT Gun
Specifications:
- Weight (approximate): 1,980 lbs.
- Length of barrel: 7 ft. 2 in.
- Muzzle velocity: 3,000 f.s.
- Weight of projectile: 3.75 lbs.

Remarks: This gun made its appearance in the German Army in 1940. It is of Skoda manufacture. The mounting is a modified Mark I tank chassis.

50-mm. AT Gun (See sketch)
Specifications:
- Weight: 1,760 lbs.
- Length of barrel: 9 ft. 10.5 in.
- Muzzle velocity: 2,953-3,280 f.s.
- Rate of fire: 16 r.p.m.
- Weight of AP shell: 4 lbs. 9 oz.
- Weight of HE shell: 3 lbs. 15 oz.

German 50-mm. Antitank Gun

Remarks: This antitank gun was issued to the main units of the German Army in the spring of 1941. It is steadily replacing the 37-mm. as the standard antitank gun. The carriage is provided with an armor-plated shield and has a tubular split trail. The AP shell has pierced the armor of British infantry tanks and cruiser tanks and our light and medium tanks. There are also reports of a 50-mm. AT gun on a self-propelled mount.

50-mm. Tank Gun (High Velocity)
Specifications:
- Weight: 421 1/2 lbs.
- Length overall: 210 cm. (12 ft. 11 in.)
- Length of chamber: 30.5 cm. (12 in.)
- Length of rifling: 162.2 cm. (5 ft. 4 in.)
- Muzzle velocity: 3,444 f.s.
- Weight of AP shell: 3.9 lbs.
- Rifling: Poly-groove plane section, uniform twist of 1 in 35 calibers, 16 lands, 3.5 mm. wide, grooves, 6 mm. wide, .75 mm. deep

Remarks: This gun is mounted in the new Mark III German tank and has been very effective.

AT Gun (M 41) (See sketch overleaf)
Specifications:
- Weight: 501 lbs.
- Muzzle velocity: 4,700 f.s.
- Caliber at breech: 28 mm.
- Caliber at muzzle: 20 mm.

Remarks: The barrel of this semiautomatic gun is constructed on the Guerlich principle, i.e., it tapers from 28 mm. at the breech to 20 mm. at the muzzle as above indicated. The gun uses the so-called arrowhead type of ammunition. The life of the barrel is thought to be not over 400 rounds. The gun has a welded carriage with a split trail. It is served by a 5-man crew. It is manufactured by the Austrian firm of Bohler.

German Antitank Gun (M 41)

II. DUAL-PURPOSE WEAPONS

20-mm. AA-AT Gun

Specifications:

- Weight in action: 1,012 lbs.
- Muzzle velocity:2,950 f.s.
- Maximum horizontal range: 6,124 yds.
- Maximum vertical range: 12,468 ft.
- Rate of fire - theoretical: 280 r.p.m.
- Rate of fire - practical: Unknown
- Elevation: 0° to +90°
- Traverse: 360°
- Length of bore: 65 cals. (4 ft. 3 in.)
- Weight of shell: 0.308 lbs.

Remarks: This gun may be towed by a light tractor or be self-propelled, mounted with a shield on a half-track vehicle. It fires self-destroying tracer ammunition. There is also a four-barreled type called the "Flakvierling." (See this publication No. 4, p. 3.)

37-mm. AA Gun

Specifications:

- Weight in action: 3,400 lbs.
- Muzzle velocity: 2,800 f.s.
- Maximum horizontal range: 8,744 yds.
- Maximum vertical range: 15,600 ft.
- Rate of fire - theoretical: 150 r.p.m.
- Elevation: -10° to +85°
- Traverse: 360°
- Length of bore: 50 cals. (6 ft.)
- Weight of shell: 1.4 lbs.

Remarks: This gun is motor-drawn or self-propelled on a half-track vehicle. It fires self-destroying tracer ammunition.

47-mm. AA Gun

Specifications:

- Weight in action: 3,400 lbs.
- Muzzle velocity: 2,620 f.s.
- Maximum horizontal range: 11,695 yds.
- Maximum vertical range: 24,000 ft.
- Rate of fire - theoretical: 25 r.p.m.
- Rate of fire - practical: 15 r.p.m.
- Elevation: -10° to +85°
- Traverse: 360°
- Weight of shell: 3.3 lbs.

Remarks: This gun originated in Czechoslovakia. It is tractor-drawn, but may self-propelled.

88-mm. AA Gun (See sketch)

Specifications:

- Weight in action: 10,400 lbs.
- Length of bore: 65 cals. (18 ft. 9 in.)
- Muzzle velocity: 2,750 f.s.
- Maximum horizontal range: 16,000 yds.

German 88-mm. Antiaircraft-Antitank Gun

- Maximum vertical range: 37,000 ft.
- Rate of fire - theoretical: 25 r.p.m.
- Rate of fire - practical: 15 r.p.m.
- Elevation: -3° to +85°
- Traverse: 360°
- Weight of shell: 19.8 lbs.

Remarks: A tactical study of the gun has been previously made in this publication; see No. 1, p. 29.

It is a high velocity dual-purpose gun equipped with a shield and has been used most effectively in the African campaigns. Its effectiveness is due to (1) mobility - towed on trailer by half track with ammunition in rear and can go into position very quickly by use of outriggers and demountable spade; (2) flexibility - (when not firing from trailer), can change from AT to AA fire in 5 to 6 seconds, traverse 360° and has specially trained crews who are able to take full advantage of its capacity to fire on rapidly moving targets; (3) high velocity - has penetrated all types of British tanks and also our own light and medium tanks.

In conclusion, the German Army has developed a system of balanced antitank protection which complements its system of antiaircraft protection. All units from the company to the division have an all-around "cubic space" (three-dimensional) protection against the greatest threats of modern warfare, the tank and the airplane.

50-MM ANTITANK GUN (GERMAN)

From the Intelligence Bulletin, February 1943.

1. GENERAL

In the summer of 1941 the German Army replaced its 37-mm antitank gun with the 50-mm, model 38. To date the 50-mm has proved one of the most effective antitank guns that the Germans have at their disposal. Armor-piercing projectiles fired in this gun weigh 4 pounds 9 ounces, and have been known to pierce the armor of British infantry and cruiser tanks as well as that of U.S. light and medium tanks. The gun has proved especially effective in jamming tank turrets by hits at the junction of the turret and hull. These hits fuze the metal of the two parts together and immobilize the turret.

This gun usually is mounted on a split-trail carriage with a shield of spaced armor plate. It is generally towed by a half-track, and has a third wheel which can be attached to the spade piece on the trail for manhandling the piece into position.

The Germans manufacture a self-propelled version of this gun. Also, the gun is commonly mounted in their Mark III tanks. When used in a Mark III tank, it can be fired electrically, instead

German 50-mm Antitank Gun.

of by percussion, and is used without a muzzle brake. The 50-mm antitank gun fires armor-piercing shells, high-explosive shells, and armor-piercing 40 shot. This last has a windshield (light, streamlined nose) and a tungsten carbide core. It gives a good armor-piercing performance at 500 yards. Incidentally, the latest type of armor-piercing shell also has a wind-shield.

2. TABLE OF CHARACTERISTICS

- Muzzle velocity (AP): 2,740fs, (AP 40): 3,940fs, (HE): 1,800fs
- Maximum range (AP): 1,540yds, (AP 40): 770yds, (HE): 2,640yds
- Effective range (AP): 1,000yds, (AP 40) : 500yds, (HE): 2,000yds
- Number of grooves: 21
- Twist: 1 turn in 32 cals
- Rate of fire: 16 rounds per min
- Total weight of gun: 1,626lbs
- Depression: 18°
- Elevation: 27°
- Traverse: 65°

3. DESCRIPTION OF COMPONENT PARTS

a. Tube

The tube is of monobloc construction with a muzzle brake attachment, and is 111.25 inches long without the breech ring.

b. Recoil System

The recoil system consists of a hydropneumatic recuperator and oil buffer.

c. Breech Mechanism

The breech mechanism is of the horizontal sliding-block type. It works semiautomatically, and also can be worked by hand.

d. Safety Arrangements

Unless the sliding breech block is properly closed, the safety

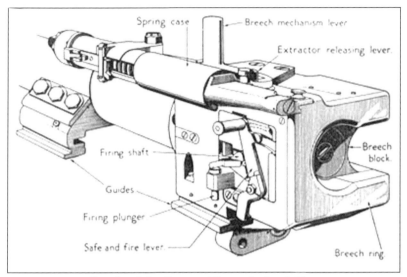

Details of the German 50-mm Antitank Gun.

plunger will not enter its recess in the lower face of the breech ring, and the gun cannot be fired.

If the safety plunger is not in its recess, the firing shaft cannot be turned.

If the firing pin is not in the cocked position, the breech cannot be opened, since the firing shaft is engaged with the safety plunger, which is in its recess.

e. Firing Mechanism

The firing mechanism is operated from the elevating gear handwheel. It is a push-button attached to a wire cable which actuates a lug on the cradle. This, in turn, actuates the firing plunger upward on to the firing shaft of the breech mechanism.

f. Sights

The firing bracket is mounted on the left trunnion, and either a telescopic sight or an open sight can be used. The sight bracket has lateral deflection gear, a range drum, and means of adjustment for azimuth and elevation. The telescopic sight is of three-power magnification.

The range drum is so calibrated that when the maximum range for armor-piercing shell (1,540 yards) is reached, the gun

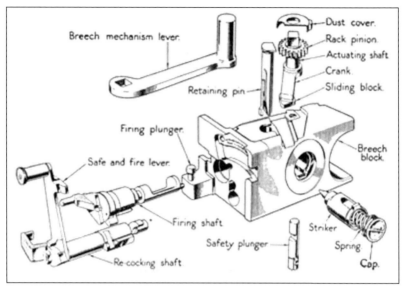

Details of the German 50-mm Antitank Gun.

automatically is sighted for high explosive, beginning with 330 yards and going up to a maximum of 2,640 yards.

g. Elevating Mechanism

The elevating gear is operated by a handwheel on the left side of the carriage. It allows 27 degrees for elevation and 18 degrees for depression.

h. Carriage

The gun has a spaced armor-plate shield composed of 2-mm to 4-mm plates about 1 inch apart. It has spoked wheels of a light alloy, with solid rubber tires. A third wheel can be attached to the spade piece so that the gun can be moved by hand.

4. AMMUNITION

Type	Weight of complete round	Length	Weight of projectile	Fuze	Identifying marks
AP tracer shell	9 lbs. 3 oz	21.4 in	4 lbs. 9 oz	Base	Black projectile.
HE shell	7 lbs. 3 oz	23.7 in	3 lbs. 15 oz	Nose	Dark green projectile.
AP 40 shot	—	—	2.025 lbs	None	Black projectile.

PENETRATION DATA

Type shell	Range	Angle	Compact	Penetration
AP shell	250 yds	30°	Plate-hardened to same degree throughout.	60 mm (2.36")
AP shell	1,300 yds	Normal	Same	60 mm (2.36")
Unconfimred on AP 40	330 yds	20°	Same	90 mm (3.54")
	440 yds	20°	Same	64 mm (2.54")

NOTE.—The above tests were fired with a limited supply of ammunition and the results probably represent underestimates.

5. CREW

The crew consists of the gun commander, No. 1 (gunner), No. 2 (loader and firer), Nos. 3 and 4 (ammunition handlers), and No. 5 (chauffeur).

A TACTICAL STUDY OF THE EFFECTIVENESS OF THE GERMAN 88 MM ANTIAIRCRAFT GUN AS AN ANTITANK WEAPON IN THE LIBYAN BATTLE

From Tactical and Technical Trends,
No. 1, June 18, 1942.

Recent cables from American military observers in Cairo and at the front with the Eighth British Army in Libya stress the important role being played by the German 88 MM anti-aircraft gun in the ground phase of the desert battles now in progress.

The effectiveness of this weapon as a tank destroyer was rather clearly apparent in the course of the November and December British Libyan offensive. One of our observers at that time stated in an official report that the 88 MM was the most feared weapon which the British tanks had to face, and that the destruction wrought by it, on both chassis and turret of the British tanks, was incomparably greater than that caused by any other Axis weapon.

The characteristics of this gun are as follows:
- Muzzle velocity: 2750 feet per second
- Weight of shell: 19.8 pounds
- Vertical range: 37,000 feet
- Horizontal range: 16,000 yards
- Weight in firing position: 5.2 tons
- The gun is tractor drawn.
- It is provided with a steel shield of unknown thickness.

An American military observer who had many opportunities to

witness this gun in Germany in 1940, speaks of this weapon as follows:

"The 88 MM is basically a gun for firing on moving targets. The crew is also specially trained for firing on highly rapid moving targets, primarily on airplanes. The whole control apparatus is designed for fast moving targets with a very rapid rate of fire: 25 rounds per minute. The gun is capable of great volume fire and extreme accuracy against moving targets of any type. It is equally efficient on targets on the ground as well as in the air. For attacks on armored vehicles, it is provided with a special armor-piercing shell."

The German 88 MM anti-aircraft gun was designed and constructed in secret in the ten year period prior to the advent of Hitler, when the German army was subject to rigid personnel and material limitations. It is known that it was the plan of its designers to construct a dual purpose anti-aircraft and anti-tank weapon. The anti-tank purpose of the weapon was, however, veiled in secrecy and the German intentions in this regard did not become known to the world until the Polish campaign of 1939.

However, so definitely was the Axis attitude offensive, not only in Poland but in the French campaign of 1940, as well, that United Nations observers did not grasp at the time the full significance and effectiveness of this weapon.

Commencing in 1940, the Germans began to provide these guns with an armored shield in order to protect its personnel against small arms bullets as well as smaller anti-tank projectiles.

It appears that this weapon has played an important role throughout the Russian campaign. However, far more exact information is available as to its use in Libya, than on the Russian battlefields.

In November 1941, when Gen. Auchinleck launched his major offensive, Marshal Rommel, his opponent, created three tank proof localities along his front line: at Bardia, Sollum and in the vicinity of Halfia pass. The defenses of each of these strong points were built around a battalion (12) of 88 MM AA guns, so sighted as to provide all around protection. These guns were supported by a large number of smaller anti-tank weapons. So well organized were these strong points that they were never seriously attacked, and only fell when the British had pushed on to Benghazi and when the water and food stocks of the strong points became exhausted. The British ascribe the long resistance put up by these strong points to the difficulty they found in coping with these dual purpose weapons.

In the battle now raging in Libya, Rommel's offensive use of these weapons is of considerable interest. The anti-aircraft guns appear to follow closely his armored vehicles. As soon as the front begins to stabilize, the 88 MM AA guns go into position and around them is then organized a "tank proof" locality. The German tanks are then withdrawn for offensive operations elsewhere.

The effectiveness of these weapons is clearly brought out from the following quotations from reports of observers now at the front in the desert battle around Tobruk:

One report includes the following statement:

"The German 88 MM guns penetrate the armour of all British tanks. British tanks dare not attack them. Up to now the British seem incapable of dealing with these weapons."

Another observer reports as follows:

"At a point in the Knightsbridge area, the 4th British armored brigade faced some 35 German tanks of the Mark III and IV type drawn up in line and obviously inviting attack. These tanks were supported by a battalion of anti-aircraft guns (12). The commander of the 4th Brigade refused to attack at all because of the presence of these guns on the battlefield.

"Slight firing occurred throughout the day. Towards evening the superior British tank force withdrew and the German tanks attacked after nightfall in a new direction. Their 88 MM guns had checked the British all day and permitted Rommel to seize the initiative as soon as the British threat had vanished."

Still a third report reads as follows:

"The greatest single tank destroyer is the German 88 MM anti-aircraft gun. For example, on May 27th at 8:00 A.M., Axis forces having enveloped Bir Hacheim, a German tank force of sixty tanks attacked the British 22nd Brigade some distance to the northeast. The British moved to attack this force with 50 light and medium American tanks. It soon became apparent that this British force was inadequate and the Brigadier commanding ordered a second regiment of 50 tanks into action. In ten minutes the 88 MM German AA guns destroyed 8 American medium tanks of this reinforcing regiment. All day thereafter, the British engaged the enemy half-heartedly and finally withdrew. Sixteen American medium tanks were lost in all. These sixteen fell victims without a single exception to the 88 MM AA gun."

PENETRATION OF GERMAN 88-MM ANTITANK GUN

From Tactical and Technical Trends, No. 8, Sept. 24, 1942.

The following penetration figures for the German 88-mm dual-purpose gun, using armor-piercing shell against armor and concrete, have been obtained from a captured German document. Angle of attack is given as 70 degrees. The quality of armor attacked is not stated, but it is believed to be of standard German specifications:

Range in Meters	Thickness of Armor (mm)	Thickness of Concrete (mm)
500 (547 yds)	71 (2.0 in)	1,100 (43.31 in)
1,000 (1,094 yds)	67 (2.64 in)	1,000 (39.37 in)
1,500 (1,640 yds)	65 (2.156 in)	900 (35.43 in)
2,000 (2,187 yds)	63 (2.48 in)	800 (31.50 in)

ARMOR PENETRATION OF GERMAN ANTITANK GUNS

From Tactical and Technical Trends,
No. 12, November 19, 1942.

a. General

The following figures show the armor-piercing capabilities of the three standard German antitank guns, the 37-mm, the 50-mm, and the 88-mm, as well as of the new long-barreled 75-mm gun which is now replacing the old short-barreled 75-mm gun on the Mark IV tank and the Sturmgeschütz (self-propelled assault artillery). These figures are based on performance of an AP projectile against homogenous armor, and supersede previously published information in Tactical and Technical Trends.

b. 37-mm Antitank Gun

Range (yards)	Penetration of Normal AP Projectile (inches)	
	(at 90°)	(at 60°)
0	2.42	1.85
250	2.17	1.63
500	1.87	1.44
750	1.67	1.24
1,000	1.44	1.06
1,250	1.26	.91
1,500	1.10	.81
Range (yards)	Penetration of Special AP Projectile (inches)	
	(at 90°)	(at 60°)
0	3.43	2.93
100	3.13	2.68
200	2.83	2.42
300	2.58	2.19
400	2.30	1.95

c. 50-mm Antitank Gun

(The new 50-mm gun in the Mark III tank has approximately the same characteristics.)

Range (yards)	Penetration (inches)	
	(at 90°)	(at 60°)
0	3.43	2.91
250	3.27	2.76
500	3.07	2.56
750	2.87	2.36
1,000	2.64	2.20
1,250	2.44	2.01
1,500	2.24	1.85

d. 88-mm Antiaircraft-Antitank Gun

Range (yards)	Penetration (inches)	
	(at 90°)	(at 60°)
1,000	4.72	4.21
1,500	4.17	3.66
2,000	3.66	3.15

e. New Long-Barreled 75-mm Gun in Mark IV Tank and Sturmgeschütz

Range (yards)	Penetration (inches)	
	(at 90°)	(at 60°)
0	4.72	3.86
500	4.25	3.50
1,000	3.82	3.11
1,500	3.43	2.76
2,000	3.03	2.44

The length of the gun is given as 43 calibers.

GERMAN TACTICS IN THE DESERT

From Tactical and Technical Trends, No. 14, Dec. 17, 1942.

The support of tanks by the other arms is essential to success of tank operations. German application of this principle is illustrated in the following information on the Axis 1942 spring offensive in North Africa.

Great alertness was shown by the German forces in covering their front with antitank guns when their tanks were halted or stopped to refuel, and in protecting their flanks at all times with an antitank screen. A threat to the German flanks by tanks was immediately met by the deployment of antitank guns while the German tanks continued their movement. The enemy appears to have a rapid "follow the leader" system of deployment and a system of visual control by means of colored disk signals.

Every effort was invariably made to draw the fire of the defense, especially the fire of antitank weapons, by the deployment and advance of a few tanks. These tanks advanced, and were then withdrawn, and the enemy concentrated his artillery and mortars on all the defenders' weapons that had disclosed themselves. After a thorough preparation of this kind, the real tank attack was launched.

In at least one instance, a passage through a minefield was cleared for German tanks in this manner: A detachment of tanks advanced to the edge of the minefield and engaged all the defending weapons they could see. Pioneers then dismounted from the tanks and proceeded to clear mines on foot, covered by the fire of the tanks. Tanks that were hit were pulled out by other tanks and then replaced.

NEW GERMAN 75-MM ANTITANK GUN

From Tactical and Technical Trends,
No. 18, Feb. 11, 1943.

With the increasing potential effectiveness of the tank, particularly in more powerful armament and greater armor thickness, there has of necessity been a corresponding development in antitank weapons. Perhaps the greatest threat to the tank is the antitank gun. Until recently the largest caliber German antitank gun (as differentiated from the AA/AT gun, or the tank gun) has been the 50-mm. It is now believed that the Germans have a 75-mm antitank gun, the 7.5-cm Pak 40. This is probably the long-barreled tank gun of the new Mark IV German tank, produced as a field piece. The importance of this development cannot be overestimated, since guns of the 50-mm class may thereby be rendered obsolescent. A further stage in the gun - vs. - armor battle may have been reached.

AMMUNITION FOR GERMAN 42-MM ANTITANK GUN

From Tactical and Technical Trends,
No. 19, February 25, 1943.

Brief mention has already been made in Tactical and Technical Trends (No. 7, p. 3) of the German 4.2-cm Pak 41 (42-mm antitank gun). This is a tapered-bore weapon, being 42 mm at the breech and 28 mm at the muzzle. High explosive and armor-piercing ammunition is provided. Both the HE and AP ammunition (see accompanying sketch) are characterized by a relatively large propellant charge and a flaring skirt or fin at the base of the projectile. The brass-coated steel shell case is 400 mm (15.75 inches) in length. The skirt of the projectile, which is squeezed down as the projectile travels through the tapered bore, serves to give a large effective base area at the commencement of shot travel. A high muzzle velocity is thus possible with a relatively light weapon. However, owing to the relatively light weight of the projectile, the velocity tends to fall off rapidly, and maximum armor-piercing performance is achieved at short ranges only. The thickness of armor penetration is considerable in relation to the weight of the gun; the hole made, is, of course, small. Barrel wear is high; just what the life of the barrel may be is not known. However, in the case of a similar German weapon, the 2.8-cm Pak 41 (antitank gun tapering from 28 mm at the chamber to 20 mm at the muzzle) the life of the barrel is thought to be not over 400 rounds. The muzzle velocity of the 42-mm is not known; that of the 28-mm is thought to be 4,700 feet per second.

As indicated in the sketch overleaf the HE and AP projectiles are similar in shape. They are sometimes referred to as

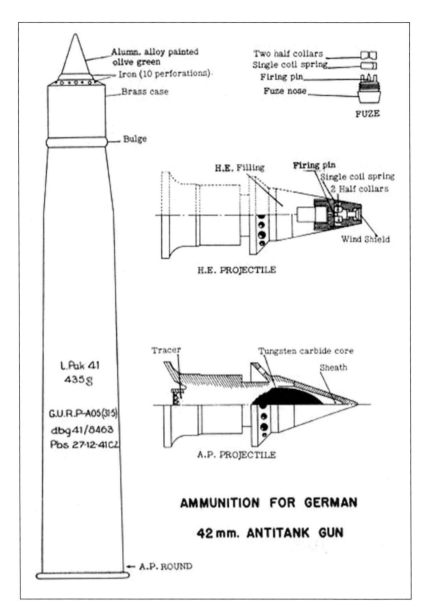

Fuze labels:
- Alumn. alloy painted olive green
- Iron (10 perforations)
- Brass case
- Bulge
- Two half collars
- Single coil spring
- Firing pin
- Fuze nose

FUZE

H.E. Projectile labels:
- H.E. Filling
- Firing pin
- Single coil spring
- 2 Half collars
- Wind Shield

H.E. PROJECTILE

A.P. Projectile labels:
- Tracer
- Tungsten carbide core
- Sheath

A.P. PROJECTILE

Round markings:
- L.Pak 41
- 435g
- G.U.R.P-A05(315)
- dbg 41/8463
- Pbs 27-12-41 CZ
- A.P. ROUND

AMMUNITION FOR GERMAN

42 mm. ANTITANK GUN

arrowhead ammunition. The perforations or holes (see sketch) are designed to decrease the mass of the skirt or fin as it is squeezed down into the recess in the projectile casing while traveling through the bore. The explosive filling of the HE projectile is blue in color, which suggests Hexagen (trimethylene trinitramine). The nose percussion fuze of the HE shell is aluminum, with the body in two sections. This fuze is of the bore-safe type; before firing, the single coil spring keeps the two half-collars squeezed against the firing pin which is thereby prevented from being depressed; in flight the centrifugal force created by the rotation of the projectile forces the two half-collars apart, and the firing pin is then free to move toward the cap on impact.

The stenciled lettering on the shell case (see sketch) has the following significance:

- First line: light antitank gun 41
- Second line: weight of propellant in grams
- Remaining lines: data on propelling charge

The HE shell case contains 310 grams of propellant and is so stenciled.

GERMAN ANTITANK AND TANK GUNS

From the Intelligence Bulletin, May 1943.

1. ANTITANK GUNS

Since 1939 the German Army has been making a tremendous effort to bring into service a satisfactory antitank gun for every type of combat unit. Even the air-borne and parachute troops have been provided with light, tapered-bore weapons. A most important development is that the German Army is no longer dependent on the German Air Force for its heavy antiaircraft-antitank gun, the 88-mm. Formerly, the Army had to borrow from the Air Force flak units armed with the 88-mm gun, because this was the only weapon which could give the requisite performance. The gun crews were German Air Force personnel, the equipment was not designed to Army specifications, and whether or not the guns were made available was likely to depend on the personalities of the commanders involved. Thus Rommel was able to get large numbers for use in a purely antitank role, chiefly because of his personal influence.

When the German Air Force releases flak units to the Army for use in an antitank role, the antiaircraft defense, which is primarily an Air Force responsibility, is bound to suffer. Hence it is only natural to expect that the Army's chief antitank weapons will increasingly be manufactured to its own specifications and will be organized as an integral part of the Army.

In the 75-mm antitank gun, model 40, the German Army now has a piece which weighs 1 1/2 tons as against the 7 tons of the 88-mm. For all practical purposes, the two guns give the same performance against armor at distances up to 2,500 yards.

Moreover, the 75-mm antitank gun, model 40, is to be manned by Army crews which have been Army-trained. In the 75-mm antitank gun, model 41, which also weighs about 1 1/2 tons, the Germans have a weapon capable of defeating, under European fighting conditions (that is, up to about 1,500 yards), armor 100 millimeters thick—and greater thicknesses at shorter ranges.

When it was first brought out, the 75-mm antitank gun, model 40, had a muzzle velocity of only 2,400 to 2,500 feet per second, and it looked as though a still more powerful weapon would have to be produced. Now, with improvements, the gun has a muzzle velocity of about 2,800 feet per second, and the performance matches that of the 88-mm.

It should be evident, therefore, that Models 40 and 41 of the 75-mm antitank gun provide a powerful combination for all ranges up to 2,500 yards. (A very recent report indicates that the Germans have introduced a new towed 75-mm gun, which has a muzzle velocity of 3,250 feet per second and which uses the same ammunition as the 75-mm antitank gun model 40.)

2. TANK GUNS

Developments in the manufacture of German tank guns have, of course, been influenced greatly by the progress of the war itself. The 1939 German tank guns were not ideal for fighting the French tanks. At first, the 75-mm gun in the Pz. Kw. 4 was intended as a close-support gun, and as such it was very successful; even now it is being used for that purpose, and has recently been mounted in some Pz. Kw. 3's and 8-wheeled armored cars. In 1941 the Pz. Kw. 3 was armed with a 50-mm weapon to fight British cruiser tanks, and the Germans decided to convert both the Pz. Kw. 3 and the Pz. Kw. 4 into fighting tanks in every sense of the term. (German tanks have always carried a generous allotment of high-explosive shells, just as German antitank guns have always been provided with high explosive shells.) As a result, in 1942 the Pz. Kw. 3 and Pz. Kw.

4 were rearmed with high-performance guns—the 50-mm Kw. K. model 39, and the 75-mm Kw. K. model 40, respectively— and were given greatly improved armor.

Moreover, two new tank guns capable of giving an even superior performance were brought into service. These guns were the 75-mm Kw. K., model 41 (tapered bore), and the 88-mm Kw. K. 36.

The appearance of the 88-mm Kw. K. 36 was probably inspired by the demand of the Afrika Korps for a gun which could throw a heavy projectile and which could give a good penetration performance at ranges of from 2,000 to 2,500 yards. The 88-mm Kw. K. 36 is a very heavy gun and one which is awkward to mount in a tank. Its ammunition (33-lb round) is hard to stow and handle in a limited space. Although the 75-mm Kw. K. 41 is a lighter gun, and uses a shorter and lighter (16 1/2 lb) round, it gives a much better armor-piercing performance than the 88-mm at any range below 1,500 yards. The 75-mm would seem to be better suited to Russian or European conditions than to desert terrain, and is likely to seen more often in the future.

The performance of the 75-mm Kw. K. does not match that of the 88-mm at any range; however, since it is fundamentally a good weapon, the Germans may attempt to improve its performance, instead of trying to develop a new and heavier gun.

3. AMMUNITION

The Germans seem to be losing interest in a combination armor-piercing, high-explosive shell, now that substantial thicknesses of armor have to be dealt with. During the past year they have been improving the anti-armor performance of armor-piercing projectiles: first, by reducing the high-explosive capacity of the heavier armor-piercing shells and, second, by continuing to develop high-velocity, armor-piercing shot with a tungsten carbide core. What this amounts to is that the Germans are

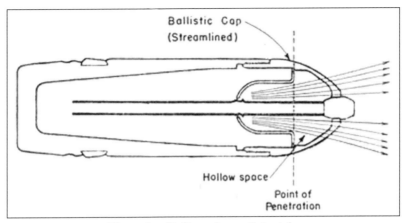

Figure 1.—Hollow-charge Principle.

employing shot for attacks against thick armor, while retaining, for every weapon, high-explosive shells to be used in attacks against "thin-skinned" targets.

The Germans now use piercing caps on armor-piercing shells for everything over 20-mm caliber.

Both the 75-mm antitank gun model 40 and the Kw. K. 40 are provided with a hollow-charge round, in addition to the high-explosive shell and the armor-piercing projectile with a ballistic (streamlined) cap. Hollow-charge projectiles have a hollow space (see fig. 1) in the nose section, to concentrate the blast against a small area and thus obtain better piercing effect. This principle is also followed in the manufacture of demolition charges and hand grenades. The Germans believe that the hollow-charge shell should not be used at ranges of more than 1,300 yards. It is interesting to note that there has been a rapid development of hollow-charge shells for all infantry, air-borne, and field artillery weapons. There is every reason to believe that the Germans will use these shells increasingly, and wherever possible.

MISCELLANEOUS (GERMAN)

From the Intelligence Bulletin, July 1943.

1. 88-MM AA/AT GUN (DUG-IN)

The drawings in figure 1 are views of a dug-in but uncamouflaged German 88-mm dual-purpose gun in North Africa.

Figure 1

GERMAN AA GUNS FOR USE AGAINST MECHANIZED VEHICLES

From Tactical and Technical Trends
No. 21, March 25, 1943.

The Germans have made extensive use of their 20-mm and 88-mm antiaircraft guns for engaging mechanized vehicles. The 37-mm antiaircraft gun, though suitable for a dual-purpose role and provided with armor-piercing ammunition, has been used to a lesser extent. In addition to these three weapons, a German document shows that the use of four other antiaircraft guns against mechanized vehicles is envisaged. These guns are:

a. 40-mm AA/AT Gun (4-cm Flak 28 Bofors)

This Bofors-design gun is generally similar to the U.S. 40-mm Bofors. Some of the particulars of this weapon are reported as follows:

- Muzzle velocity: 2,950 f/s
- Length of bore: 60 cals
- Max. horizontal range: 12,300 yds
- Effective ceiling: 16,200 ft
- Weight of projectile (HE): 2.2 lbs
- Rate of fire (practical): 80 rpm
- Weight in action: 1.9 tons
- Weight in traveling position: 1.9 tons
- Elevation: -50 to +90°
- Traverse: 360°

b. 50-mm AA/AT Gun (5-cm Flak 41)

Little is yet known of this weapon, which was introduced in December 1940, except that it fires both HE and AP, is an automatic weapon, and is produced in either mobile or fixed models. The sight fitted is Flakvisier 41, which is operated by one man and is described as a completely automatic clockwork sight.

There is a possibility that this may be a tapered-bore gun, as the only two other German guns designated with the number '41' (the 2.8-cm Pak 41 and the 4.2-cm Pak 41) have been of the tapered-bore type.

c. 83.5-mm AA Gun (8.35-cm Flak 22 (t*))

This is a Skoda gun introduced into the Czech Army in 1922 as their standard semimobile heavy AA gun. Particulars are:

- Muzzle velocity: 2,625 f/s
- Length of bore: 55 cals
- Max. horizontal range: 19,650 yds
- Max. vertical range: 39,250 ft
- Weight in traveling position: 8.4 tons
- Elevation: 0° to +90°
- Traverse: 360°
- Weight of projectile (HE): 22.4 lbs
- Tractor drawn

Abbreviation for "tscheck," meaning Czech.

d. 105-mm AA Guns (10.5-cm Flak 38 and 39)

This gun is a standard heavy AA gun. It was originally designed as a dual-purpose antiaircraft-coast-defense gun. Experiments were made to produce the gun in a mobile form, and a limited number on mobile mounts appeared at Hitler's birthday parade in 1939. This mount was said to be unsatisfactory, and the gun was used as a fixed model only for a time. Recent reports indicate, however, that a new mobile mount has been provided, and it is reported likely that the Germans intend using the weapon in antitank role as they do the 88-mm gun. Particulars are:

- Muzzle velocity: 2,890 f/s

- Length of bore: 60 cals
- Max. horizontal range: 19,075 yds
- Effective ceiling: 36,700 ft
- Rate of fire (practical): 8 - 10 rpm
- Weight in action: 11.56 tons
- Elevation: -3° to +85°
- Traverse: 360°
- Weight of projectile (HE): 33.2 lbs
- Types of ammunition: HE with time fuze
- HE with percussion fuze
- AP shell
- Tractor-drawn on a 4-wheeled carriage.

GERMAN 75-MM ANTITANK GUN

From Tactical and Technical Trends
No. 22, April 8, 1943.

In case any of the 75-mm Pak 97/38 guns fall into the hands of our artillery, it should be a fairly familiar weapon. The gun is a long-barreled adaptation of the French "75" with some interesting modernizations. Noteworthy are the double shield with an air space between the two plates, the perforated Solothurn muzzle brake, the odd-looking split trail, which would seem to give a large and rapid traverse, and the third smaller wheel set under the trail spades. This third wheel can be folded up flat on top of the trail. The carriage is quite similar to the 50-mm German antitank gun. With a screw breech-block like the old "75;" the piece is typically French. An earlier type of French 75-mm dual-purpose antitank-field piece, said to fire a 14.1-pound solid shot at 2,100 f/s velocity, was completed in March 1940. The present weapon appears to be a development of this gun.

GERMAN ANTITANK UNITS IN REARGUARD ACTION IN AFRICA

From Tactical and Technical Trends No. 22, April 8, 1943.

According to reliable reports, the tactical use of antitank weapons by German units operating on rearguard missions, is as follows: First, the 88-mm dual-purpose guns fall back, then the combat engineers, and the antitank guns last. Unless the attack is too overpowering, the antitank units, before withdrawing, stand fast for a length of time designated in orders. If the gun positions are undetected, antitank fire is opened only at the last possible moment, since the German 50-mm guns are not effective against General Grant (U.S. M3) and General Sherman (U.S. M4) tanks at long ranges. If the gun positions are known to the enemy, long-range fire is employed.

ANTITANK TACTICS AS SEEN BY U.S. COMBAT PERSONNEL

From the Intelligence Bulletin, July 1943.

The following comments on German antitank tactics in Tunisia are from members of a U.S. armored division. It is believed that these descriptions of the enemy in action will be of interest and value to junior officers and enlisted men.

1. A BATTALION COMMANDER

German antitank gunnery in Tunisia made our reconnaissance a particularly tough job. The Germans dragged up their big 88-mm guns and dropped them in position behind their tanks. Usually a crew dug its gun in a hole 12 by 12 by 6 feet deep, virtually covering up the shield and exposing only the barrel of the gun. We found these guns especially hard to locate. (In fact, they can break up your whole show if you don't pick them up in time.) Apparently the Germans used mats to hide the muzzle blast. Once we hunted three days for a gun, which was within 1,000 yards of us, and then found it only by spotting the personnel approaching the gun position.

Generally, the Germans tried to suck us into an antitank-gun trap. Their light tanks baited us in by playing around just outside effective range. When we started after them, they turned tail and drew us within range of their 88's. First, they opened up on us with their guns in depth. Then, when we tried to flank them, we found ourselves under fire of carefully concealed guns at a shorter range. We've just got to learn to pick off those guns before closing in.

When the Germans went into position, they hid their guns and tanks in anything available, including Arab huts. Then they dressed their personnel in Arab garb so that these men could go to and from their positions. Usually the Germans tried to draw us within a 1,200-yard range. They frequently used machine guns to range themselves in, and we ducked their shells by watching that machine-gun fire. When they were moving, they shot at anything that looked suspicious, and generally knocked down every structure in sight. (We thought this a good idea, and followed suit.) Sometimes the Germans got the range with high-burst smoke shells. But when we saw three of those in a line, we took off. We had discovered that it was the high sign for the Stukas.

One evening several Mark IV's followed a British tank column right up to their tank park until a 25-pounder battery spotted the strangers on the tail of the column and blew them off the road.

Later the lieutenant-colonel was asked a question about the use of tanks in action. He said:

The Germans towed their 88's behind their tanks. (Maybe they brought up 75's, or both; I know they brought up 88's.) They towed them up and dug in. Their tanks came out and attracted our attention, and, until we caught on to their tricks, the tanks led us right between the guns, got behind us, and gave us the works. We learned not to form the habit of going for the first 88's which shot at us. There were likely to be several much closer up. The first 88 that barked and the first tank were generally bait, and we had to refrain from plunging at them. When they staged any night attack or late evening attack, and neither side pressed the fight, the Germans put their 88's in No-Man's-Land way ahead of where their tank positions were. In one instance their tanks were within 1,000 yards of a pass, but their guns were 4,000 yards ahead of the pass.

"Four 88's, if dug in, are a match for any tank company. They are the most wonderful things to camouflage I have ever seen. They are very close to the ground. You can watch the fire coming in; little dust swirls give the guns away and show how low they are. The projectiles just skim over the ground. The pit is 12 by 12 by 6. The gun looks like a pencil or black spot. The shield is level with the piece, and all you can really see is the tube. In Tunisia the crews, dressed in Arab clothes, did everything they could to camouflage positions. Our artillery found that it could get them out with high-explosive. When a tank gun could find them, it could get them out, too.

Over 1,200 yards there was no use in worrying about the 88. Its fire bounced off our medium tanks at that range. Under 1,200 yards, we took care to watch out. His gunnery stank at long ranges. In general, I felt that our men were better.

We soon learned to pick off the leader of a tank group. After a while we were able to tell which was the leader, because of certain differences in behavior. When we got one of their commanders, the other tanks stopped and seemed sort of dazed.

One day I had an interesting experience. Ten German tanks were sitting on a ridge, shooting at half-tracks. They had been at my left rear and I hadn't seen them. There were Mark IVs, some Mark IIIs, and a Mark VI. They stopped on the crest and did a right flank and started to get in column. The Germans sometimes put a Mark VI in the middle and the others on the flanks—-always making one flank heavier than the other, however. We picked out one and hit him, and he stopped. We burned the next one. Then the Mark VI, which I had thought was a Mark IV, came close. The Mark VI tanks are hard to identify, but have a more or less square outline with an offset box on the side. We bounced four rounds off the front of him. Then another tank came up right along side of him, and it was easy to move a hair's breadth to the left and pick him off. (We had no AP, so I know an HE will crack a Mark IV. You should shoot low, and it will ricochet and kill them in the turret, or damage them so they will be of no use.) We had to move out of it when the Stukas appeared.

Whenever Stukas came along, the German tanks sent up

colored flares to identify themselves. Then, with three smoke shells, they marked a target for the Stukas.

The Germans used a lot of high-burst ranging. I noticed that the artillery was likely to fire a round, apparently getting the range from the map, and get one overhead and then drop right down on us. It was comparatively easy to dodge an 88, because they started with machine-gun bullets. When they began hitting us, we moved suddenly to the right or left to avoid the fire.

2. A COMPANY COMMANDER

When you fire on the German tanks, they play a lot of tricks. When we fired on them in Tunisia, they stopped, leading us to think that we had knocked them out. When we turned around on something else—wham, they opened up on us!

It would really be worth your time over in the States to shoot at your men at night with tracer bullets. In Tunisia the Germans used tracers and sometimes raised hell with our troops. Tracers throw a hell of a scare into you, anyhow; each one looks as though it's headed straight for you. The Germans are cracker-jacks at night fighting, I might add.

I'm also concerned about another question of tactics, which is probably none of my business. We had always been taught that the Germans attacked at dawn or in the early morning light. Actually, just to confuse us, they were even more apt to hit us at dusk, when there was only half an hour of light left in the sky. Then they threw everything they had at us—including their star shells and Very lights—in an attempt to put us on the run.

3. A TANK COMMANDER

I think that a battalion of infantry trained to operate at night could slip into a German tank park and really raise hell. One night, after we had been burned out of our tank during action, we made our way to within 30 yards of a parked tank, thinking it was an Arab hut. The Germans don't seem to worry so much about security at night.

The September 1943 Intelligence Bulletin contained the following correction:

In Intelligence Bulletin, Vol. I, No. 11, p. 29, par. 3, a U.S. Army officer was quoted as saying: "Over 1,200 yards there was no use worrying about the 88. Its fire bounced off our medium tanks at that range." It has since been established, however, that German 88-mm guns constitute a danger to U.S. medium tanks at any range up to 5,000 yards.

GERMAN ANTITANK MAGNETIC CHARGE

From Tactical and Technical Trends,
No. 23, April 22, 1943.

Until a technical analysis reveals a detailed breakdown of the functional operation of this device, a practical, field analysis, made in the Middle East, is given in this report with a sketch which is not to scale.

a. The Grenade

It is painted field gray. The magnets attached to the base of the charge are said to be strong enough to hold it against a vertical surface. The total weight is about 6.5 pounds—the magnets themselves weighing about one-half the weight.

The main filling (1) is contained in a pressed metal container. The neck (2) performs the dual function of forming a hand-grip and also contains a recess (3) for the detonator. A screw-threaded closing cap (4) is set above internal screw-threads (5) which receive a BZE igniter (see description below of this igniter). Six bolts (6) tie the base of the conical portion to the magnets. Between the magnets and base of the conical portion is the

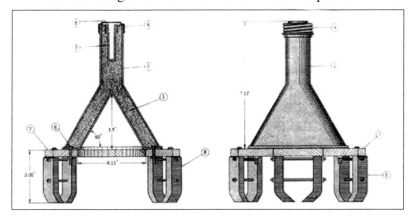

plywood framework (7). There are three horseshoe magnets (8).

Additional information obtained from enemy sources further serves to identify what is apparently the same grenade. The grenade is called Hafthohlraum Granate (clinging hollow-space grenade); it is funnel-shaped, and adheres to an enemy tank by magnetic attraction. It was said to be first employed on the Russian front in July 1942. These grenades are either transported in cardboard containers or else suspended from the soldier's belt.

In using the grenade, it is reported that the soldier moves forward towards a tank, via the "dead area" where the tank is unable to reach him with its fire. Upon reaching the tank, he places the grenade against the hull where it adheres through magnetic attraction. The fuze is pulled at the same time. Meanwhile, the grenade holds fast to the metal for several hours.

The destruction is caused by simultaneous melting of the metals and by destructive explosion.

The funnel-shaped body of the grenade is made of thin steel. The incendiary material is described as a pink dust which, when ignited, gives off a terrific heat—sufficient to burn through the armor plate almost immediately. Heat is accompanied by an explosion and the emission of choking gases.

b. BZE Igniter

(1) General

This is the standard igniter for the German egg-shaped grenade, it may also be used with demolition charges and booby traps. The head (5—see sketch) is painted blue; this igniter has a delay of about 4 1/2 seconds. However, there is a similar igniter with a head colored RED which has a delay of only 1 second. The latter is used with the so-called German "shaving sick grenade" (used as a booby trap) and a signal smoke flare; when used with these, the igniter cannot be easily removed because of the locking nut on the underside of the lid of the container, but they are reasonably safe to handle once the igniter has been neutralized.

It is important to note that it has recently been reported from North Africa that German egg-shaped grenades have apparently been booby-trapped with the 1-second delay igniter; if the red cap is removed and the firing cord pulled the grenade detonates almost instantaneously.

(2) Description

The BZE igniter consists of a brass body (1), which contains the friction composition through which the pull wire (2) is drawn. The lower end of this wire is coiled (3) to provide the resistance to the pull. The upper end of the wire has a loop through which is fastened one end of a cord 2 1/4 inches long. The other end of the cord is attached to a disk (4) inside the spherical head (5). As the head is unscrewed and pulled, the slack in the cord will be taken up when the disk catches in the opening of the head. Pull is then exerted on the wire, the friction composition is ignited, and in turn ignites the compressed powder in the steel tube (6).

(3) To Neutralize

(a) If the igniter is found with the head in place, it is safe to handle without further manipulation.

(b) To render the igniter inoperative, carefully unscrew the head, taking care not to exert any pull on the cord.

(c) Cut the cord by means of scissors and replace the head with the cord inside.

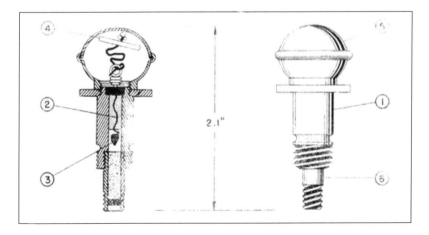

GERMAN CLOSE-IN TACTICS AGAINST ARMORED VEHICLES

From Tactical and Technical Trends, No. 23, April 22nd 1943

The following is a translation of a German document issued early in 1942. While some of the methods of attack discussed may have since been altered, it is thought that it reflects the essentials of current German doctrine. The preface explains the scope and purpose of the document.

Current Instructions For Close-in Tactics Against Armored Vehicles

Preface

These directives are based on experiences of the German Army in close-in combat against Russian tanks on the Eastern Front. The Russian tactics so far as known have been taken into consideration.

New doctrines of our own are in process of development and will be available to the troops after completion, together with directions as to their use. First, the Eastern Army will be equipped with incendiary bottles. Presumably the troops at the front use means of fighting about which, at the time of publication of these directives, no description is yet at hand. In addition, new enemy methods will appear, which will be adapted to our own fighting.

These directives, therefore, present only preliminary instructions. Cooperation of the troops in the field is needed for their completion. To this end, new fighting practices of our own and of the enemy should be reported, with drawings and descriptions of battle conditions at the time. Communications should be sent through the service channels to the General of Infantry and to the General of Mobile Troops in the Army High Command.

The importance of close-in fighting against tanks makes it imperative that individual tank hunters be trained immediately in all the arms. The state of training in the Reserve Army will be tested by recruit inspections.

These directives apply to combat against all kinds of armored vehicles. For simplification, only tanks are mentioned in the text.

I. General

1. If there are no armor-piercing weapons at hand, or if their fire does not show sufficient result against attacking tank forces, specially trained, organized, and equipped tank hunters will have to assault and destroy tanks by close-in combat, making use of their special assault weapons and without waiting for specific orders. All other available arms will lend their support as strongly as possible.

Experience proves that with proper training and skilled use of close-in weapons, all classes of tanks can be destroyed by individual soldiers.

2. Close-in combat against tanks demands courage, agility, and a capacity for quick decision, coupled with self-discipline and self-confidence. Without these qualities, the best combat weapons are of no use. Proper selection of personnel is therefore of decisive importance.

3. Thorough knowledge of enemy tank types and of their peculiarities and weaknesses in battle and movement, as well as complete familiarity with the power and use of our own weapons in every terrain, is necessary for successful combat. This will strengthen the self-confidence of the troops. It will also make up the crucial points in training.

4. Close-in combat against tanks may be necessary for all situations and all troops.

In the first place the combat engineers, and tank hunters are the mainstays of this type of fighting. It must be demanded that each member of these arms master the principles and weapons of close-in antitank combat, and that he use them even when he does not belong to an antitank squad.

5. Over and above this, soldiers of all the armed services should be selected and grouped into close-in tank-hunting squads consisting of one leader and at least three men. They must continually be ready for close-in combat with tanks.

Where special close-in weapons are not at hand, expedients should be devised.

Combining tank-hunting squads into tank-hunting groups may be useful under certain conditions.

6. The equipment for close-in tank hunting consists of the following: incendiary bottles and Tellermines, TNT, automatic weapons (our own or captured), submachine guns, Very pistols, hand grenades, smoke bottles, and camouflage material, as well as hatchets, crowbars, etc., to use as clubs for the bending of machine-gun barrels projecting from the tank. Of this equipment the useful and available weapons for blinding, stopping, and destroying the tank should always be carried along. In the interest of maximum mobility, the tank-hunting soldiers must be free of all unnecessary articles of equipment.

II. Combat Principles

7. Careful observations of the entire field of battle, early warning against tanks, as well as continuous supply and readiness of tank-hunting equipment of all kinds and in ample quantity, will insure against surprise by enemy tanks and will permit their swift engagement.

8. It should be standard procedure continually to observe the movements and the action of tank-hunting squads and to support them by the combined fire of all available weapons. In this connection, armor-piercing weapons must direct their fire on the

tanks while the remaining weapons will fight primarily against infantry accompanying the tanks. It will be their mission to separate the infantry from the tanks.

Sometimes tanks carry infantrymen riding on them, who protect the tanks at forced or voluntary halts against the attack of tank hunters. These security troops must be destroyed by supporting infantry before the tank hunters attempt to assault the vehicles. Should the tanks arrive without infantry, the fire of all the available weapons will be concentrated against the vulnerable places of the tank. The shorter the range and the more massed and heavy the fire, the greater the physical and moral effect.

Fire by sharpshooters is always of special value.

The activity of tank-hunting squads should not be hampered by the supporting fire. The mission of such supporting fire is to split up tank forces, to blind and put the crews out of action, and to have a demoralizing effect on them, thereby creating favorable conditions for close-in assault.

In case fire support by other weapons is impossible, the attack by tank-hunting squads must proceed without it.

9. The basic principles of close-in assault are the same in all battle situations. In defense, knowledge of the terrain and of the time available will be profitable for the preparation and the attack.

10. The carrying out of close-in combat will largely depend on the immediate situation. The number, type, and tactics of the attacking tank force, the terrain, our own position, and the effect of our own defensive fire will always vary, and this variation will demand great adaptability and maneuverability on the part of our tank hunters.

11. Only one tank can be assaulted by a tank-hunting squad at one time. If several tanks attack together and if only one tank-hunting squad is available, then that tank is to be assaulted which at the moment appears as the most dangerous or whose

engagement promises the quickest success. In general, the choice must be left to the tank-hunting squad.

If there is a sufficient number of squads available, it is advisable, particularly in defense, to hold one or more squads ready in the rear for the destruction of tanks which may break through.

12. Generally speaking, the procedure will always be: first, to blind the tank, then to stop it, and finally to destroy the vehicle and the crew in close-in combat.

13. Whether the tank-hunting squads advance at the beginning of a tank attack or whether they leave their foxholes only during the engagement or whether the whole assault goes on from under cover depends entirely on the situation.

The behavior of the squads depends on whether the tank is moving or is voluntarily or involuntarily halted.

The attack on a heavy or super-heavy tank will often be easier than on a light tank, because the former in general is clumsier and has poorer observation. But the destruction of heavy tanks generally demands the use of more powerful weapons.

14. It is important in every case to make full use of the dead space around each tank.

In general, tanks should be attacked from the side or the rear. Any moment of weakness of the enemy tank should be utilized (i.e., impeded vision, halts, climbing and overcoming of obstacles, etc.).

15. Tanks should be approached by crawling and stalking, making full use of cover and concealment.

16. The foxholes of tank hunters must be narrow and have steep walls. They must be built without parapets and must not be recognizable by enemy tanks. They may be camouflaged either by canvas strips or branches. Whenever possible they should be protected by a belt of mines.

17. The tank hunters will remain motionless in their foxholes observing their targets and waiting in readiness for the favorable

moment to assault. They must face the enemy tank calmly and must have the nerve to "let it come." It is always wrong to run away. While moving, the single soldier is inferior to the tank. In hiding, on the contrary, he is usually superior. He is safest inside the dead area around the enemy tank.

In villages, close-in assault of tanks is usually easier than in open terrain because of the abundant possibilities for hiding and cover (as by roof-snipers).

Often the corner of a house, a bush, or a fence are sufficient as hiding places.

By the use of obstacles of all kinds, dummy mines and guns, and signs like "Warning — mines!", enemy tanks may be guided into terrain unfavorable to them, but favorable for the assault squads and antitank weapons.

18. When attacking moving tanks, the tank hunters at first must be well concealed and permit the tank to come close to them (7 to 20 meters); then they try to stop the tank by blinding it, or at least they force it to slow down. A strong blinding effect is obtained through the massed fire of all weapons. By using explosive charges, tank hunters destroy the tracks of the tank and cripple it. They will then assault it and destroy it and its crew with their close-in weapons.

In the case of halted tanks, the squad stalks up on it using the terrain to its best advantage.

19. Around every tank there is a dead area which it cannot cover with its principal weapons. The higher a tank, the larger, usually, is its dead space. In general, this space has a radius of about 20 meters (see figure 1 overleaf). To combat targets in the dead space, tanks have slits through which pistols and submachine guns can be fired. Frequently a machine gun is found on the rear side of the turret.

When assaulting a tank, the tank hunters must make use of the dead space. They should approach the tank from the direction which is opposite to the direction of its principal weapons. This

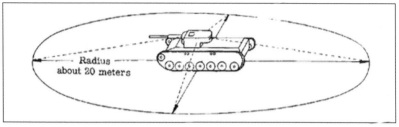

Figure 1

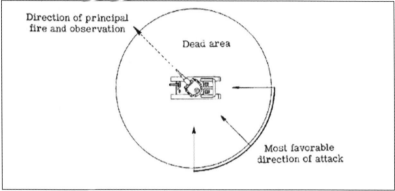

Figure 2

is also opposite to the direction of its principal observation (see figure 2). Should this approach be impracticable because of a machine gun in the back of the turret, the squad will attack from the side or diagonally from the rear.

20. The tank hunter with the principal close-in weapon will use it against the tank while the other tank hunters support him with their fire. Should he be impeded by that fire, it must cease. When the crew of the tank becomes aware of the assault, they will open the turret hatch so as to defend themselves with hand grenades. That instant will be used by the observing tank hunters to fire against the open turret and to wound the crew. Crews of stalled or burning tanks who do not give themselves up when getting out will be destroyed in close combat. If the tanks are still undamaged, they are made useless by removal of the breech-blocks, by destroying the machine guns, and by setting fire to the gasoline tanks.

21. Neighboring units support the attack by rifle and machine-

gun fire against the vision slits of the attacking tanks as well as against accompanying infantry which might endanger the tank hunters. The tanks are blinded and prevented from taking accurate aim, and the enemy infantry is forced to take cover. Weak places of the tank are taken under fire with armor-piercing ammunition and antitank weapons. Lead-sprays entering through the shutters into the inside of the tank will wound the crew. The cooperation of the tank-hunting squads with other troops in the area must be previously arranged, and all signals decided upon.

III. Close-in Combat Weapons and Their Use

22. There are several kinds of short-range media (blinding, burning, and explosive) which allow many variations of use. The type of armored vehicle, its position, and the terrain determine which of the available weapons are to be used, or if several should be combined. The leader of the tank-hunting squad will have to decide quickly which medium to adopt under the circumstances.

According to the doctrine "Blind, halt, destroy," the tank-hunting squad has to be equipped with blinding, explosive, and incendiary materials. Explosives have the double purpose of stopping and destroying the tanks.

Blinding Agents
Smoke Candles and Smoke Grenades

23. Smoke candles or several smoke hand grenades, thrown in front of the tank with allowance for wind direction, minimize its vision and force it to slow up.

Smoke

24. Common smoke is used like smoke from candles. To be able to obtain it at the right moment, distribute straw or other highly inflammable material in the probable avenue of approach, drench it with gasoline or kerosene, and ignite it with signal rockets at the approach of tanks.

The detonation of grenades and artillery shells also creates clouds of smoke. Moreover, the firing of armor-piercing grenades against the vision slits promises success.

25. When smoke is used, the tanks are hidden also to our antimechanized weapons, and they are unable to aim accurately. Therefore, smoke should be used only when the vehicles have come so near that they cannot be covered by fire any longer without endangering our own troops, and therefore have to be destroyed at close range.

Signal Rockets

26. Signal rockets shot against vision slits have a blinding effect, particularly at dusk and in the dark; also, the vehicle is illuminated for our antitank weapons. Note that signal rockets only begin to burn at a distance of 25 meters.

Covering of Vision Slits

27. For this purpose one man jumps onto the tank, preferably from the rear, or approaches the tank closely from the side, and covers the vision slits or periscopes with a blanket, overcoat, shelter half, etc., or applies mud, paint, or grease. This is possible only if the tank is moving slowly or is halted, and if it is not protected by the fire from other tanks or following infantry. Any tank crew will be strongly demoralized by the presence of an enemy on top of their tank.

Incendiary Agents

Flame-throwers

28. Flame-throwers are aimed at vision slits, weapon openings, ventilators, and engine cover.

Incendiary Bottles

29. Incendiary bottles are a combat weapon used against tanks, armored scout cars, and other cars. In street and house fighting, they can also be used against living targets. They are thrown against the front part of the tank for blinding purposes, over the engine for incendiary purposes.

The contents of an incendiary bottle (not self-igniting) are 2/3 gasoline and 1/3 fuel oil. Ignition of the incendiary bottles takes

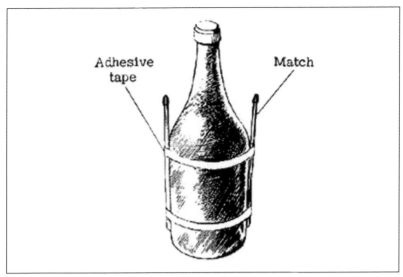

Figure 3

place (when it has broken after hitting a hard surface) by the use of special safety matches.

The incendiary bottles are packed in wooden boxes in damp sawdust. The boxes also contain adhesive tape for fastening the matches to the bottles. The safety matches are packed in batches of twenty with 3 scratch pads in containers of noninflammable material. Two safety matches are taped to the bottle. The heads of the safety matches can be pointed either toward the neck or to the bottom of the bottle (see figure 3). The matches are lighted immediately before throwing the incendiary bottle, by friction with any rough surface or the match box. See that both matches are burning properly.

The bottles can be thrown in two different ways; throwing by swinging the arm, holding the bottle at the neck (see figure 4 overleaf), or throwing by pitching, like putting a shot, grasping the bottle at its heaviest point (see figure 5 overleaf).

Either of the two ways is practicable. In general, the position of the thrower will determine the type of throw. In a prone or similar position he will not be able to swing his arm, and therefore will have to pitch it. Whenever possible it should be

Figure 4

Figure 5

thrown like a stick hand grenade, because the accuracy of aim is greater and the possible range will be increased.

The most vulnerable parts of a tank are: the engine (ventilation — on tanks usually in the rear), the vision slits, and imperfectly closed hatches.

Should an incendiary bottle miss and remain intact, it is better to leave it until the matches have burned out, as the heightened pressure might cause an explosion. The bottles should be handled with care. They should not be bumped together or against hard objects.

Improvised Incendiary Bottles

30. Any bottle can be filled with an inflammable liquid, preferably mixed with wool fiber, cotton, or torn rags. A good mixture is two-thirds gasoline and one-third oil. Note that Flame-oil #19 is not freeze-proof. A mixture of gas and fuel oil can be used instead.

To ignite it, the bottle is equipped with an improvised lighter. It is constructed in the following way:

A wick is passed through a hole in the cork of the bottle, so that one end hangs in the liquid. To the free end are attached several matches. Several wicks may also be used without the cork, if they completely close the opening of the bottle and are well drenched in the fluid (see figure 6).

At the approach of the tank, the wick is lighted and the bottle thrown. When it breaks, the fluid is ignited by the wick and is distributed over the tank and its engine. Generally the tank catches fire. If further bottles are thrown against the tank, they do not have to be ignited before throwing. Even initially a bottle without an ignition device can be used. After breaking the bottle on the tank, the liquid can be ignited with signal rockets, hand grenades, smoke candles, smoke grenades, burning torches, or

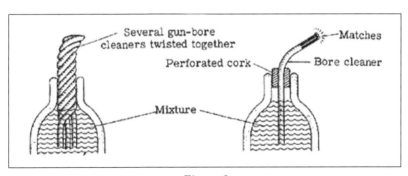

Figure 6

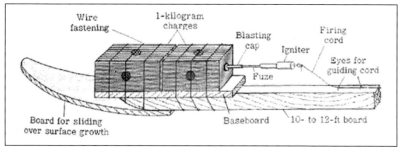

Figure 7

burning gasoline-drenched rags.

Captured Enemy Incendiary Bottles

Bottles with a self-igniting phosphorus mixture (so-called Molotov cocktails) are used as explained in paragraphs 29 and 30. If large numbers of these weapons are captured, they should be collected and reported, to enable distribution among as many troops as possible.

Gasoline

32. Several quarts of gasoline are poured over the engine housing of the tank, and ignited as in paragraph 30. Gasoline can also be poured into a tank. It is then ignited by a hand grenade which is also pushed in.

Hand Grenades

33. Quite frequently an enemy is forced to open the hatch for better observation. This opportunity can be used to throw grenades in a high arc into the interior of the tank. The crew can thus be eliminated and the tank set afire. Sometimes it may be possible to open the hatches with crow bars or bayonets and throw grenades into the interior.

Smoke Candle or Smoke Grenade

34. When thrown (as in paragraph 33) into the interior of the tank, they start the tank burning, or at least force the crew to get out because of the thick smoke.

Signal Rockets

35. Signal rockets shot into open hatches with a Very pistol can also start a tank burning.

Explosives

Hand Grenades

36. Several hand grenades can be combined into one concentrated charge (see paragraph 38).

One-Kilogram Blasting Slab

37. A slab of 1 kilogram [2.2 pounds] of explosive, placed on top of a tank, has about the same strength as a concentrated charge of 7 hand grenades and gives the crew a severe shock. Two such concentrated charges damage the turret hatch considerably and for a short time make the crew unable to fight because of the high concussion. Two or three such charges combined into a multiple charge can so severely damage the tracks of tanks that they will soon break under use. Even better are two such concentrated charges combined into an elongated charge. For this purpose, two to three 1-kilogram charges are tied to a board with wire and equipped with a short piece of fuze (see figure 7).

To destroy machine-gun and cannon barrels protruding from the tank, two 1-kilogram charges are tied together, hung like a saddle over the top of the barrel, and detonated (see figure 8). Machine-gun barrels are torn by the explosion, and cannon barrels bent sufficiently so that an attempt to fire the gun will completely destroy it. Inserting hand grenades into the muzzle of the guns also has good results against cannon and crew. Shells will also burst in the barrel if stones, wood, or earth are rammed

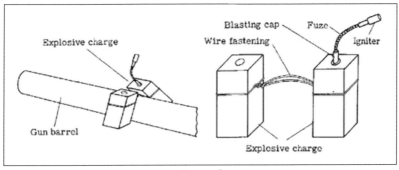

Figure 8

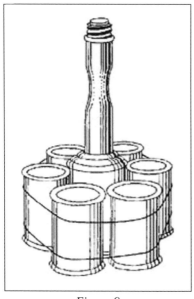

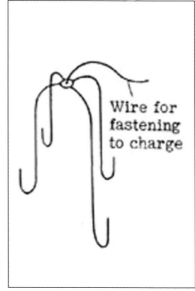

Wire for fastening to charge

Figure 9   *Figure 10*

into it. Placing hand grenades in the vision slits is also effective.

Several 1-kilogram charges can be tied together as a field expedient in case of lack of finished multiple charges.

Concentrated Charges

38. The bodies of seven stick grenades are tied together securely with wire so that they will not fall apart when used. Only the middle grenade is fitted with the usual handle with an internal igniter (see figure 9). This charge is ineffective against the armor or tracks of heavy tanks. But the concussion of the charge, exploded on top of the tank, will be so strong that the crew will be knocked out temporarily.

39. The concentrated charge of 3 kilograms, is found ready for use in the infantry engineer platoon, infantry engineer platoon motorized, engineer companies, and engineer battalions.

It will pierce about 60 mm of armor and is best placed over the engine or the driver's seat. The crew will be badly wounded by small fragments of the inner walls spattering off. The concussion is unbearable. To destroy the tracks, the charge must fully be covered by them.

Even greater effect will be obtained by combining several 3-kilogram charges.

40. The throwing radius for a concentrated charge is 10 to 15 yards. When throwing it, the soldier must consider the length of the fuze (about 1/2 inch burns in 1 second). The thrower aims at the tracks or at the belly of an approaching tank.

41. The concentrated charge can also be used as a multiple charge or as a slide-mine as described in paragraph 37 above.

42. If the charge is supposed to be used on top of the tank it must be secured so it will not fall off. For this purpose, its bottom is painted with warmed tar. If the charge is primed, be careful! A charge thus prepared will adhere to horizontal and even to slightly inclined surfaces. Putty can be used also for this purpose, but it is not reliable on wet surfaces.

Charges may be held on a tank by using an anchor made of strong wire, which is hooked into openings or protuberances of the vehicle (see figure 10).

43. The ignition for paragraphs 39 to 41 is provided by preparing short fuzes with detonating caps (to burn in 4 1/2 to 15 seconds), time fuzes, prima-cord, and wire for improvised pull igniter, or a pressure-igniter. The latter fastening is best suited for the destruction of tracks.

If the charge is thrown, a short fuze is needed (but at least 4 1/2 centimeters long, like a hand-grenade fuze). If it is placed on the tank, a 15-cm fuze is used for the security of the man placing it. [1 centimeter of fuze burns in about 4 seconds.]

Sliding Mines

44. Charges of 3 or 6 kilograms can be made and built into a two-sided skid. This sliding mine has to be secured against premature detonation, resulting from falling or turning over, by the insertion of two woodblocks (figure 11 overleaf).

Two to four sliding mines are linked together and at each end of a given group is a 20-meter cable or rope.

Tank hunters sit in two foxholes about 20 meters apart. The

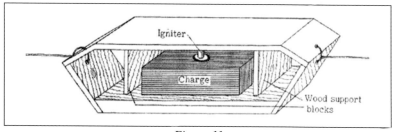

Figure 11

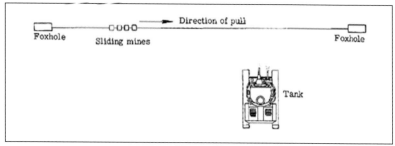

Figure 12

sliding mines are camouflaged and placed somewhere between the holes so that they can be pulled in either direction. At the approach of a tank, they are pulled under its tracks (figure 12).

Several pairs of soldiers in similar foxholes can protect a larger area, for instance a key-point of resistance (figure 13).

Tellermines

45. Instead of concentrated charges, Tellermines [antitank mines] can be used, either as multiple charges or as sliding mines. However, as they have a high radius of fragmentation, they can only be worked from splinter-proof positions.

IV. Close-in Combat with Firearms

46. There should always be close cooperation between the tank-hunting squads and the other combat elements in the area. Discussion between the leader of the tank-destroyer squad and the leader of the other available arms is advisable in order to fix the beginning and end of the fire attack against a tank.

47. New [Russian?] tanks have especially strong armor at some points. But they have many weak spots, against which even the fire of weapons which are not armor-piercing can be

successful. It is therefore imperative to hit the tank not only as a whole, but especially at those weak spots.

48. For this purpose, it is necessary that the rifleman, conscious of the power of his weapon and of his superiority over the tank, should keep cool. He must be able to open fire on the tank as late as possible, surprising it at the shortest possible distance. Courageous riflemen with rifle or antitank rifle, making full and skillful use of terrain, should crawl up to the best range.

The shorter the range, the greater the accuracy of the weapon. Also, the armor-piercing capacity of the ammunition will be increased.

When using armor-piercing ammunition, in order to ensure its successful use, it is important to follow closely the instructions found in the ammunition boxes concerning the aiming points and the effective range.

Opening fire as late as possible has the further advantage of keeping the weapon concealed from covering tanks and observers up to the decisive moment.

49. Frequently it will be advisable to concentrate the fire of several similar or different weapons on one tank e.g., rifles, a light machine gun, a heavy machine gun, an antitank gun, and a light infantry cannon. Ambush-like concentration of all weapons to surprise the tank is preferable. The physical and moral effect

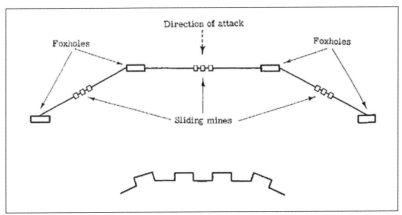

Figure 13

will be heightened by such concentration. If only a few tanks appear, it is preferable to assault them successively according to the danger presented by individual tanks. In the case of a massed attack, rigid fire control must insure that the most dangerous tanks are attacked simultaneously.

50. When several different weapons are combined against it, the tank will be blinded by the use of heavy machine-gun fire and small explosive grenades. At the same time, guns of 75-mm caliber and larger will fire against the tracks to cripple the tank. It is necessary to wait for a favorable moment, when for instance difficult terrain slows up the tank, or when it halts to fire. Once it is stopped, it will be destroyed by combined fire or by close-in assault.

51. Weapons with armor-piercing ammunition of smaller calibers are sometimes ineffective against tanks with sloping armor plates, even if their power of penetration would be great enough to pierce the plate if vertical. Because of the slope of the plates, the ammunition ricochets from the tank. On such tanks it is necessary to aim at the vertical parts.

Even in the case of vertical armor plates there will be an oblique angle of impact if a tank approaches at a sharp angle. In that case the angle of impact is also such that the projectiles will ricochet. Therefore, the tank should be fired upon at right angles. If the tank appears at an unfavorable angle, firing will be withheld until it assumes a more vulnerable position, either by revolving the turret or by actually turning and maneuvering.

52. It is possible to increase the effect and accuracy of fire by the selection of a flanking position, because the tanks are usually less strongly armed on the sides, and also offer a bigger target. Furthermore, vertical armor is more common on the sides than on the front.

53. Weak parts of tanks, against which fire from all arms is effective, are: vision slits, openings for hand weapons, periscopes, hatches, shutters, turret rings, ventilator openings,

track, belly (the part of the hull between the tracks), and the engine cover (usually in the rear). The accurate location of these parts in the individual types can be found in the manuals.

54. Severe physical and moral effect can be achieved with the rifle, the light machine gun, and the heavy machine gun by firing heavy ball ammunition and armor-piercing ammunition at less than 300 yards against the weak parts of the tank, or by firing with submachine guns and armor-piercing grenades from a grenade discharger at very close range.

Projectiles hitting the vision slits or periscopes blind the crew, and prevent them from aiming or driving accurately. Also, small particles of molten lead and lead fumes penetrate into the interior of the tank and may injure the crew. Some bullets might jam the turret ring or weapon shutters so that revolving of the turret or firing the weapons will be made impossible.

As tanks are more poorly armored on top, attack from high points such as trees or houses will get better results.

The demoralizing effect on the crew of the noise of bullets hitting the tank surface should not be underestimated.

55. HE and armor-piercing grenades (impact fuzes) fired with the rifle grenade-launcher (flat trajectory), antitank guns up to a caliber of 50-mm, the 75-mm infantry howitzer, and the 150-mm infantry howitzer directed against the weak parts of a tank will have about the same results as described in the preceding paragraph. Furthermore the power of impact will cause the inside surface of the armor plates to splinter off and wound the crew. If the projectiles have high explosive charges like the heavy infantry howitzer, the crew will become casualties from the concussion, or they will be at least temporarily knocked out.

When firing against the engine cover in the rear with explosive shells of all weapons, an incendiary effect may be obtained under favorable circumstances. Light and heavy infantry howitzers attack the tracks most effectively.

The ranges for individual weapons have to be selected so that great accuracy of aim can be achieved. For small dispersion and flat trajectory the light and heavy infantry howitzers should use the maximum charge.

The turret, the side, and the rear of the tank are considered weak parts for armor-piercing ammunition. Armor-piercing weapons, unable to use armor-piercing ammunition, can effectively assist in the assault against tanks with high-explosive ammunition.

57. Destructive results in combat against armor are obtained with the 37-mm stick grenade or bomb. Its short range, however, results in success only at close distances.

V. Training

58. Training in close-in attack on tanks includes the knowledge of the weak parts, of the construction, use, and effect of close-in weapons, and of combat principles. To this purpose, instruction (using sand-table models and captured enemy tanks) and practical exercises are necessary. After the individual fighter has been trained, the cooperation of the squad and group in terrain exercises will be practiced. Combat exercises with live ammunition against large dummies or captured tanks will complete the training.

59. To improve accuracy in antitank fire, riflemen and gunners of all the arms (machine gun, antitank, infantry howitzer, field artillery) must know all vulnerable parts against which their weapons can be used effectively, and they must perform daily aiming exercises against tank models. Special practice is needed for the use of the Very pistol and rifle grenade. By the use of sub-caliber fire with antitank guns and practice firing with rifles and machine guns against tank models, and by combat exercises, marksmanship is to be developed to the utmost.

60. Each rifleman, whether he is part of a tank-hunting squad or the gunner of an individual weapon, must be thoroughly

convinced that, if he fights skillfully he and his weapon are superior to any tank. He has to know that he is the hunter and the tank the game. This thought is to be given great weight in the training period.

VI. Assault Badge

61. The destruction of tanks in close-in combat counts as an assault. Rifemen, tank hunters, and other personnel who have fulfilled the necessary requirements in destroying tanks, will be awarded the assault badge.

GERMAN 75-MM ANTITANK GUN—7.5-CM PAK 40

From Tactical and Technical Trends
No. 25, May 20, 1943.

Mention of this gun has already been made in Tactical and Technical Trends (No. 18, p. 4). It must not be confused with the 7.5-cm Pak 97/38 which is a German modification of the well-known French 75 (see Tactical and Technical Trends, No. 22, p. 6).

The 7.5-cm Pak 40 is very similar in appearance to the standard German 50-mm antitank gun, the 5-cm Pak 38. However, the following structural differences may be readily noted:

Item	5-cm Pak 38	7.5-cm Pak 40
Shield	Curved. Flattened at outer edges	Angular. Flat frontal section with two flat side pieces set at an angle of approx. 45° to the plane of the frontal section
Muzzle brake	Narrow and elongated	Broad and longer
Sighting aperture	Rectangular	Square

The gun proper, i.e., exclusive of the carriage, is essentially the same weapon as the 7.5-cm Kw.K 40, which is the principal armament of the new German medium tank, the PzKw 4. Two self-propelled versions of the 7.5-cm Kw.K 40 have also been reported, one mounted on the chassis of a PzKw 2, the other on the chassis of the PzKw 38 (t). The chief differences between the 75-mm antitank gun and tank gun are probably the substitution of mechanical firing and percussion primer for electric firing and primer; the chamber of the antitank gun is also probably considerably longer. The breechblock is the semi-automatic, horizontally sliding type.

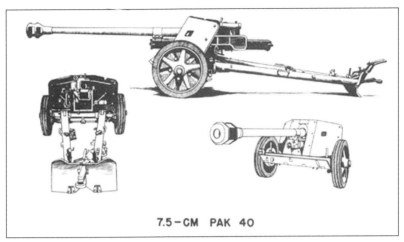

7.5-CM PAK 40

5-CM PAK 38

The piece is mounted on a split-trail carriage, with torsion springing; this springing is automatically cut out when the trails are opened. The wheels are of a light alloy and are fitted with solid rubber tires. An interesting feature is a detachable third wheel which can be fitted on near the trail spades, thereby permitting the gun to be man-handled more easily. The shield is of the spaced-armor type like the Pak 38; note also that a protective apron is provided.

Further details on this weapon are as follows:

- Over-all length in travelling position:19 ft 2 in
- Weight in action: 3,350 lbs
- Length of barrel: 10 ft 6 in
- Length of recoil: 35.43 in
- Elevation: 22 degrees
- Depression: 5 degrees
- Traverse: 65 degrees

Four types of ammunition are used, namely HE, hollow charge, AP shot, and an armor-piercing tracer shell with a small explosive charge and an armor-piercing cap covered with a ballistic nose. Details on this latter type of ammunition (see sketch opposite) are these:

- Weight of complete round: 27 lbs
- Length of complete round: 36.14 in
- Weight of projectile: 15 lbs
- Weight of HE filling: 3/4 oz
- Weight of propellant: 6 lb 3/4 oz
- Muzzle velocity (estimated): 2,830 f/s

With this AP-HE ammunition it has been estimated that this gun can penetrate homogeneous armor as follows:

Range	Normal	30 degrees
500	5.20 in	4.43 in
1,000	4.72 in	4.02 in
1,500	4.27 in	3.62 in
2,000	3.82 in	3.23 in
2,500	3.43 in	2.87 in

The AP shot is the usual German steel casing enclosing a tungsten carbide core; it is fitted with tracer. The muzzle velocity with this ammunition is reported to be 3,250 feet per second.

Comment: Detailed confirmed information on the effectiveness of this weapon is not available as yet. For its size it does have a low silhouette, a desirable feature for an antitank gun. While the muzzle velocity is high, the tube is of monobloc construction and the propellant charge is very large, so that the safety factor is open to question. The Germans have been doubling the length of the chambers in their tank and antitank weapons (e.g., the Russian 76.2-mm gun), and seem to have reached the conclusion that it is worthwhile since they are now producing this 75-mm antitank gun with the long chamber and shell case as a standard weapon.

94

DEVELOPMENT OF GERMAN TANK AND ANTITANK GUNS

From Tactical and Technical Trends
No. 26, June 3, 1943.

A detailed analysis of the chronological development of German tank and antitank guns is presented in the following report, which is preceded by an examination into the basic requirements for tank and antitank guns. All of the information contained in this article comes from British sources.

a. Theory

In order to bring into proper perspective the various lines of German antitank and tank gun development, it may be useful first to consider various factors which influence design, and to consider also the effect of design on both actual performance and lethal or destructive effect.

(1) The Problems of the AT Gun

The principal requirements for an antitank gun are the following:

(a) Ability to perforate the enemy's tank armor at the maximum range at which accurate engagement can take place;

(b) A projectile which will not only penetrate the armor but cause sufficient mechanical damage inside the tank, or personnel casualties, to disable the tank as a fighting vehicle;

(c) Ease of maneuver and concealment, requiring a carriage and a total weight which will permit speed into and out of action, and a low silhouette;

(d) A high rate of fire, a flat trajectory, and an accurate sight to enable it to engage relatively small and moving targets;

(e) Protection for the gun crew against machine-gun fire as a minimum, and against AP and HE projectiles and bomb near-misses as an optimum;

(f) An HE projectile which will enable the gun effectively to engage soft-skinned targets, when the opportunity offers and does not conflict with the gun's primary task.

(2) The Problems of the Tank Gun

Insofar as a tank gun under modern conditions is expected to be able to deal with enemy armor, most of these same conditions will apply, with an additional condition imposed by the need for economy of space in a tank.

(3) The Problems of Projectiles

(a) General

The ability of a projectile to penetrate armor depends to a great extent on the velocity at which it strikes the target, and to a lesser extent on its weight and on the angle at which it strikes. It follows, therefore, that given equality of projectile design, material, weight, and angle of strike, the higher the muzzle velocity at which the projectile is fired, the greater the thickness of armor which will be penetrated at a given range.

It also follows that given equal muzzle velocity and quality of projectile design and material, the heavier the projectile the less the penetration performance will decrease as range increases, since the heavier projectile maintains its speed through the air better and the descending curve of remaining velocity is flatter.

The heavier the projectile, the more difficult it becomes to achieve in practice a high muzzle velocity without being forced by mechanical considerations to heavy guns and bulky ammunition. Hence the antitank gun-designer is immediately faced with several problems. Is he prepared to accept a light projectile with a high muzzle velocity, relatively rapid deceleration, loss of striking power at longer ranges, and relatively slight lethal effect, in order to be sure of penetrating thick armor at the shorter ranges? If he is, he will have to take a chance on securing a direct hit on a vital spot to get results.

Is he prepared to accept a lower scale of penetration at the shorter ranges with a heavier projectile, which will, however, keep up its performance better, and do more damage at extreme ranges wherever he gets a hit? And if he decides to take as his target a thickness of armor of X inches, which no normal antitank gun of manageable proportions will defeat, how is he going to get the extra velocity to drive his projectile through it?

(b) A German Solution: The Tapered-Bore Gun

In general, increased velocity can be obtained in three ways: by increasing the pressure in the gun behind the projectile, by lengthening within limits the bore of the gun (and consequently the travel of the projectile under pressure), or by increasing the area of projectile upon which a given pressure acts. The first method increases the weight of the gun; the second also gives an unmanageable barrel for field purposes (for instance, a 3-inch high-velocity gun, using suitable propellant, might require a barrel length of about 100 calibers, or 25 feet); the third tends to give a projectile of bad ballistic shape. The tapered-bore or Guerlich design adopted by the Germans for certain of their weapons employs the third method, but gets over the disadvantage mentioned by gradually reducing the base area of the projectile as it travels through the bore, thus bringing it to a proper ballistic shape by the time it leaves the muzzle.

With the Guerlich design they have managed to produce guns of light weight capable of penetrating exceptional thicknesses of armor at the shorter ranges of engagement. For this performance they have had to sacrifice a great part of the destructive effect inside the tank. A projectile from a straight-bore weapon of, for instance, 3-inch caliber weighs about 15 pounds, and in penetrating the armor not only throws into the tank large pieces of disrupted armor from a 3-inch hole, but follows through either intact, or in fairly large fragments, to cause widespread damage. On the other hand, the projectile from a tapered-bore gun of the same entrant caliber weighs only about 6 pounds and will emerge as slightly less than 2 1/4-inch caliber. Owing to its design it will only force a hole of about 1 1/4-inch diameter in the armor, and owing to the material of the core, internal damage will be restricted to that done by small fragments within a fairly narrow cone opening out from the point of impact.

It must also be borne in mind that with high velocity (i.e., greater than about 3,500 f/s muzzle velocity), it is necessary to employ a tungsten carbide core to enable the projectile to give full penetrative value for its high velocity. The necessary raw material (wolframite) is not in such generous supply that the wholesale arming of every antitank gun with such a projectile could be contemplated.

In the event of a hit failing to penetrate, damage done by the light high-velocity projectile will be negligible compared with that caused by the equivalent normal projectile. However, taking everything into consideration, the tapered-bore gun is potentially a very serious threat to the heavier armor, particularly if a succession of hits can be obtained; but if only one hit is obtained, the probabilities of causing immediately disabling damage are relatively low. It is not a weapon which can, with advantage, engage in long-range duels with any adequately armed tank.

It would not for instance prove profitable in the open African desert, where duels at ranges of up to 2,500 yards are common, but in the close conditions of some European countrysides it might find all the conditions for its profitable employment satisfied. In more open conditions, the normal straight-bore weapon with its heavy projectile will have every advantage.

With a tapered bore, effective engagement of soft-skinned targets is difficult of fulfillment. High performances with both AP and HE projectiles from the same gun are incompatible, and while it is possible to compromise with a normal straight-bore weapon, losing a bit each way, there can be no compromise with a tapered-bore antitank gun, and HE performance must be sacrificed.

b. Developments

The rapidity with which the German forces have expanded and developed their tank and antitank armament is among the outstanding technical performances of this war. New weapons have appeared in quick succession, in turn to be superseded or improved, and throughout there has been a parallel development and improvement of ammunition.

At the end of 1939, the German Army had one standard antitank gun, the 37-mm Pak. To supplement this, they had to call on the heavy antiaircraft equipment, the 88-mm Flak. They had tank guns of 1934 vintage, the 20-mm Kw.K 30, the 37-mm Kw.K, and the 75-mm Kw.K. The antiarmor performance of tank guns was low.

Early in 1941, the German Army had, in addition to the 37-mm Pak, a new 28-mm tapered-bore, light antitank gun, the Pz.B 41, primarily for airborne troops and infantry, and a new 50-mm antitank gun, the 50-mm Pak 38. As a stop-gap, the Czech 47-mm antitank gun was also being used. The 37-mm Kw.K had been dropped from their tank armament, and in its place came a moderately effective 50-mm tank gun, the 50-mm Kw.K.

In addition, early in 1942 the German Army had put to use as an antitank gun the Russian 76.2-mm field gun, of which considerable numbers mast have been captured. This was the first heavy antitank gun under the control of German ground forces. The antitank armament of airborne troops had been considerably strengthened by the introduction of a new tapered-bore gun, the 42-mm Pak 41, which tapers to 28 mm at the muzzle. The 50-mm tank gun used in 1941 was replaced by the long-barrelled 50-mm Kw.K 39 based on the very successful 50-mm Pak 38. An improved 20-mm gun, the Kw.K 38, had been provided for light tanks and armored cars, though later models of some of these have the 50-mm Kw.K 39.

The tables below show the remarkable change in the hitting

power of their armament. The guns listed under 1939 were those then in use; those under 1941 and 1942 first appeared in these respective years.

Antitank Guns	
1939	37-mm Pak (2,500 f/s)
1941	37-mm Pak (obsolescent)
	28-mm Pz.B 41 (4,580 f/s)
	47-mm Pak (t) (2,540 f/s) (Czech)
	50-mm Pak 38 (2,700 f/s)
1942	37-mm Pak (obsolete)
	42-mm Pak 41 (4,500 f/s)
	50-mm Pak 38 (2,700 f/s)
	76.2-mm Pak 36 (r) (2,200 f/s) (Russian)
	75-mm Pak 97/38 (2,100 f/s) (French)
	75-mm Pak 40 (2,800 f/s)
	75-mm Pak 41 (4,000 f/s)

Tank Guns	
1939	20-mm Kw.K 30 (2,600 f/s)
	37-mm Kw.K (2,500 f/s)
	75-mm Kw.K (1,350 f/s)
1941	20-mm Kw.K 30 (2,600 f/s)
	50-mm Kw.K (2,500 f/s)
1942	20-mm Kw.K 38 (2,600 f/s)
	50-mm Kw.K 39 (2,700 f/s)
	75-mm Kw.K 40 (2,400 f/s)
	88-mm Kw.K 36 (2,600 f/s)
	75-mm Kw.K 41 (4,000 f/s)

Ammunition		
1939	1941	1942
AP shell	AP shell	A.P.C.* shell
HE shell	A.P.C.B.C.** shell (1.25% HE)	A.P.C.B.C. shell (.31% HE)
	AP 40 shot	AP 40 shot
	HE shell	HE hollow charge shell
		HE shell

Armor-piercing capped with ballistic cap (British abbreviation).
**Armor-piercing capped (British abbreviation).*

c. Comment on Latest Developments

(1) Antitank Guns

It is quite clear that since 1939 a very great effort has been made to bring into service an efficient antitank gun for every type of combat unit. Even the airborne and parachute troops have had special provision made for them in two light tapered-bore weapons. Most important of all, the Army is now no longer dependent on the GAF for its heavy antitank weapon.

The Army had to obtain from the GAF, on loan, Flak units armed with the 88-mm gun, because it was the only gun in the German service with the requisite performance. The gun crews were GAF personnel, the equipment was not designed to an Army specification, and whether they were made available or not depended in some cases on the personality of the two commanders involved. The GAF for their part has had undoubtedly to suffer pressure from time to time with a view to their releasing Flak units to the Army, and to the employment of these units in a purely AT role to the detriment of AA defense, mainly a GAF responsibility. However, the multi-purpose AA/AT weapons were retained.

The Army must have insisted on having its main antitank weapons produced to its own specification and organized as an integral part of the Army. They now have the 75-mm Pak 40, which weighs about 1 3/4 tons in action as against almost 5 tons for the 88-mm, has the same performance against armor up to 2,500 yards as the 88-mm, can be produced with greater ease, and will be manned by Army crews. In the 75-mm Pak 41, which also weighs about 1 3/4 tons, they have a weapon which will give them performance adequate to defeat, under European fighting conditions (i.e., up to 1,500 yards), any homogeneous armor not thicker than 100 mm, and correspondingly greater thickness at shorter range.

As originally produced, the 75-mm Pak 40 only had a muzzle velocity of 2,400 to 2,500 f/s, and it seemed as if a still more powerful weapon must be developed. Now, however, this gun has been modified; a muzzle velocity of about 2,800 f/s is obtained, and armor-piercing performance is up to that of the 88-mm Flak 36. Therefore, this weapon, along with the 75-mm Pak 41, provides a very powerful combination for all ranges up to 2,500 yards. The Germans may well decide to leave occasional super-heavy tasks to the divisional 105-mm guns and the 105-mm Flak of the GAF. This should not be taken as meaning that they will not proceed with the development of a still heavier antitank gun, but rather that production will probably for the present year, be concentrated on the 75-mm equipment. Any heavier antitank gun may well take the form of an improved 88-mm multi-purpose gun with higher muzzle velocity and a suitable field mounting. (Sketchy reports of an 88-mm Flak 41 much more powerful than the Flak 36 are now starting to come in.)

(2) Tank Guns

Since 1939 a radical change of policy is evident. The 1939 tanks, insofar as gun-power was concerned, could barely fight against the French tanks. The short-barreled 75-mm gun in the PzKw 4 was intended primarily as a close-support gun. Even today it is being used in that role, and has recently been mounted in some PzKw 3 tanks and 8-wheeled armored cars. It should be noted that German tanks have always carried a considerable amount of HE. The killing of soft-skinned targets and antitank guns is always a consideration in their policy.

In 1942 the PzKw 3 and PzKw 4 were rearmed with high-performance long-barreled guns, the 50-mm Kw.K 39 and the 75-mm Kw.K 40, respectively.

These two new guns, together with the 75-mm Kw.K 41 (tapered bore), and the 88-mm Kw.K 36, suggest an interesting line of policy. The demand from the German Army in Africa was undoubtedly for a gun throwing a heavy projectile and keeping its penetration performance up over 2,000 to 2,500 yards. This appears to have been met by the provision of the 88-mm Kw.K 36 mounted on the PzKw 6.

It is doubtful whether the Germans would accept desert conditions, in which so small a proportion of their forces were engaged, as a basis for their major weapon-production program. They are more likely to base this on Russian and European conditions. This seems to have led them to the 75-mm Kw.K 41, a lighter gun with a shorter and lighter (16 1/2-lb) round, but with an armor-piercing performance markedly superior to the 88-mm at any range below 1,500 yards.

The performance of the 75-mm Kw.K 40 is not as good as that of the 88-mm Kw.K 36 at any range, but it is probable that having here a good gun, they will aim at improving its performance.

(3) Ammunition

There has been a marked tendency in the past year to improve the anti-armor performance of AP projectiles, first by reducing the HE capacity of the heavier AP shell, and second by the continued development of high velocity shot with tungsten carbide core. This suggests that a compromise armor-piercing explosive projectile is not acceptable now that substantial thickness of armor has to be dealt with. The latest design of the 75-mm A.P.C.B.C. projectiles has so low an HE capacity as to suggest that this projectile has been included because their troops have become used to a shell that will burst inside the tank, and sudden elimination of the base fuze and explosive feature might worry them. In other words, the Germans are for practical purposes using shot for the attack of thick armor, and retain for every weapon HE for the attack of soft-skinned targets.

It also seems clear that they have been expecting the Allies to go to face-hardened armor, or else they decided some time ago that a piercing cap so improves the performance against any type of armor that the extra production time is justified, since there are now no uncapped AP projectiles in production for anything above 20-mm caliber.

It is a fact that both the 75-mm Pak 40 and Kw.K 40 are provided with hollow-charge in addition to the A.P.C.B.C. and HE, with the expressed intention that the former should not be used for extreme ranges for the reason that it is a low-velocity projectile.

There is every reason to believe that these shells would be of great use against heavily armored pillboxes, armored vehicles, and tanks, because of the "cavity charge" effect.

GERMAN USE OF AT GUNS WITH TANKS

From Tactical and Technical Trends,
No. 27, June 17, 1943.

An American army observer in Tunisia reports that German tanks habitually operate in conjunction with AT guns, as has long been their practice. The employment of these weapons is not always the same, but when units encounter enemy tanks they should expect AT guns. One German maneuver wherein the enemy launched a flank attack with tanks against our forces is described as follows (see sketch):

As the enemy armor drove into the flank, its objective our supporting artillery and then our infantry, AT guns, including 88-mm, were "peeled off" and went into position to protect the German tanks from the counterattack of our tanks and/or tank destroyers.

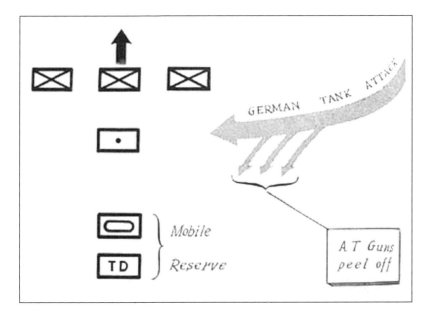

On other occasions the Germans used their often-tried stratagem of sending forward a number of tanks which would then withdraw in an attempt to lure our armor into range of their AT weapons. This is the same stratagem which the Germans used with such success against the British tanks during the heavy fighting prior to the British withdrawal to the El Alamein line in June 1942.

A GERMAN ANTITANK GUN EMPLACEMENT

*From Tactical and Technical Trends,
No. 28, July 1, 1943.*

Asketch of a German diagram of an emplacement for an antitank gun shows some interesting details. The diagram is stated to have been prepared for a defense system based on defense areas. The German document in explanation thereof follows.

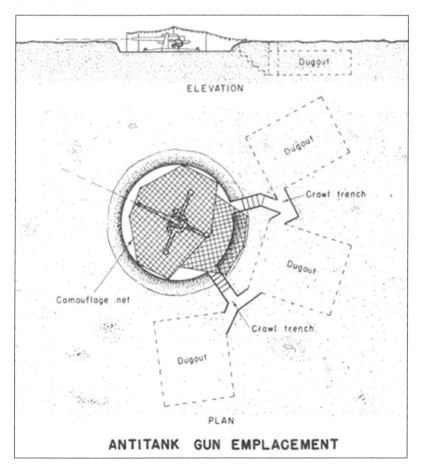

ANTITANK GUN EMPLACEMENT

"The positions will be arranged in accordance with the following plan:

(a) Field of fire in all directions;

(b) The crew as near as possible to the gun;

(c) Two to three men in one dugout with the dugouts mutually interconnected;

(d) Crawl trenches to the position. This will allow firing in any direction; enable the crew to be ready for action at all times; and permit the men to move about unobserved even during the day."

GERMAN 88'S IN TUNISIA

From Tactical and Technical Trends,
No. 28, July 1, 1943.

A battalion commander of a U.S. tank regiment which saw a lot of action in Tunisia is the source of the following observations on the tactical use of German 88-mm AA/AT guns against tanks and other vehicles.

German antitank gunnery has made our reconnaissance a particularly tough job. They drag their big 88-mm guns (maybe 75's as well—I know they bring 88's) up behind their tanks and drop them in position. Usually the crew digs the gun in a hole 12 by 12 by 6 feet deep, practically covering up the shield and exposing only the barrel of the gun. They are the most wonderful things to camouflage I have ever seen. They are very low to the ground. You can watch the fire coming in; little dust balls on the ground give them away and show how low they are. The gun looks like a pencil or black spot. The shield is level with the piece and all you can effectively see is the tube. Apparently they use mats to hide the muzzle blast. When the Germans go into position they'll hide their guns and tanks in anything, including Arab huts. They dress their personnel in Arab garb while going to and from their positions. We've found these guns particularly hard to locate, and they can break up your entire show if you don't pick them up in time. Once we hunted a gun within a thousand yards for 3 days, and then only found it by spotting the personnel approaching the gun position.

Generally the Germans try to suck you into an antitank gun trap. Their light tanks will bait you in by playing around just outside effective range. When you start after them, they turn tail and draw you in within range of their 88's. First they open up on you with their guns in depth. Then when you try to flank them you find yourself under fire of carefully concealed guns at a shorter range. Don't always bite at the first 88's which shoot at you. There will be several up much closer. The first 88 that barks and the first tank are generally bait. If they stage a night attack or late evening attack, and neither side stays on the battlefield, they will come out and put their 88's in no-man's-land away ahead of their tank positions. In one instance their tanks were within 1,000 yards of a pass, but their guns were 4,000 yards on the other side. Usually the Germans will try to suck you inside of a 1,200-yard range. Over 1,200 yards there is no use in worrying about their antitank fire because it will bounce off the medium tank at that range. Under 1,200 yards, watch out. Their gunnery stinks at long ranges. I feel that our men are better. The Germans frequently use machine guns to range themselves in, and you can duck their shells by watching that machine-gun fire. When they're moving they'll shoot at anything that looks suspicious and they'll generally knock down every Arab house in sight. Sometimes they'll get the range with high-burst smoke shells; three of these in a line is the high sign for the Stukas.

GERMAN TELLERMINES

From Tactical and Technical Trends,
No. 28, July 1, 1943.

L and mines are not a new development, but their use in astronomical numbers, as in recent campaigns, is new to this war. The mine is normally associated with war at sea. But the pre-eminence of the tank, or "land battleship," in battles on land has emphasized the importance of the land mine and made its use mandatory around any well-defended position. Among the most widely used antitank mines is the German Tellermine. The four known models of this mine are described below.

a. Tellermine No. 1

The 1935 model or Tellermine No. 1 is circular in plan with a diameter of 12 3/4 inches. It has a convex top, a flat bottom, and a maximum height of 3 1/4 inches. The total weight of the mine is 19 1/4 pounds. In a fully armed condition the mine is equipped with a main pressure igniter in the center of the top cover, and one or two standard pull igniters in its base as secondary firing devices. The principal features of this mine are shown in the accompanying sketches (figure 1). The body of the mine is a circular metal box (1) with a dome-shaped top surface containing 11 pounds of high-grade pressed TNT. A "floating" cover (2) is held down by a heavy metal ring (3) attached to the body and is supported in the center by a heavy spring (4). The spring fits into and bears on a metal fitting (5) which fits into the top of the body. The fitting also acts as a receiver for the detonator (6). Directly above the detonator are the two metal collars (7) and (8) (which screw into a recess in the fitting), a compressible rubber ring (9), and the igniter (10). The lower collar (7) is a retaining collar for the detonator; the upper collar (8) is an

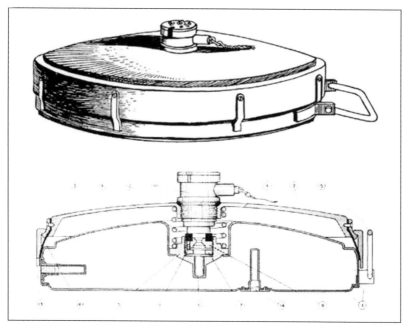

FIG. 1

adjusting or positioning collar for the igniter. The compressible rubber ring serves as a cushioned seat for the bottom of the igniter. The upper collar is screwed into the proper position in the fitting by means of a special tool. The small, headless set-screw (11) holds the collar (8) in position. The igniter is screwed into the mine cover (2) until it bears firmly on the rubber washer (12) and the rubber ring (9). The body of the mine has two receptacles (13) and (14), threaded to receive secondary firing devices. One receptacle is usually located in the side of the body opposite the handle, and the other in the bottom between the handle and the center of the mine. The mine has a metal carrying handle (15). A rubber strip (16) seals the junction between the cover and the body of the mine against the entry of water and dirt. The washer (12) seals the joint between the igniter and the cover.

b. Tellermine No. 2

This mine thought to be the 1942 model, is similar in size to the

112

1935 model or Tellermine No. 1. Its main dimensions are:

- Maximum diameter (at base): 12.75 in
- Maximum height: 4.1 in
- Diameter of pressure plate: 5.7 in
- Total weight of mine (filled): 19.3 lb
- Weight of filling (TNT plus three penthrite detonating charges): 12.0 lb

The mine consists of a body (1) (see figure 2) fitted to a circular base plate (2). The base plate is turned over along its edge to make a press fit over the flange of the body as indicated at (3). A carrying handle (5) is attached by means of a T-strip (4) which is welded to the body.

The mine is fitted to take two additional igniters. One is located in the side of the mine 4 inches from the handle at (6), and the other is in the base of the mine at (7). The pocket or

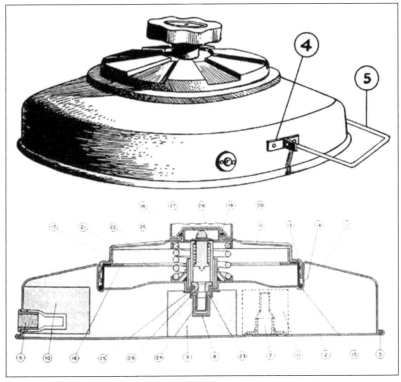

FIG. 2

receptacle (8) for the main detonator protrudes into the mine filling, and is surrounded by a cylindrical penthrite detonating charge (9). Cylindrical penthrite detonating charges (10) and (11) also surround the screwed-in pockets for the additional igniters. The details of these detonating charges are as follows:

Detonating charge at	Length	Diameter	Weight
(9)	1.6 in	2.38 in	0.36 lbs
-10	2.3 in	1.6 in	0.25 lbs
-11	1.6 in	1.6 in	0.11 lbs

The pocket or receptacle for the base igniter (7) is fastened to the circular base plate (2), its center being 2 1/4 inches from the center of the base plate. The base plate is pressed on and crimped to the circular body (1) without regard to maintaining a fixed position for the base igniter relative to the main igniter-detonator assembly. As a result, the base igniter may lie with its center at any point on the perimeter of a circle with a radius of 2 1/4 inches from the center of the base plate (i.e., also from the center of the main igniter-detonator assembly). This should always be borne in mind in searching for the position of the base igniter. The pressure plate (12) is held in the body by means of the collar (13), which is a spring fitted into the recess. The pressure plate has a rubber skirt (14) which fits into the depression (15), so that when assembled the operating mechanism under the pressure plate is protected from the entrance of dust and moisture. The rubber is held between the rim of the pressure plate (12) and the flat ring (16) spot-welded in several places to the ring (17); the latter is in turn spot-welded to the pressure plate.

The pressure plate is shaped to prevent local collapse and is closed at the center by the screwed plug (18) with a rubber seal (19). The igniter tube (20) is spot-welded into the center of the recess in the mine body, and around it is placed the loose collar (21) which holds in position the pressure spring (22). The screwed collar (23) secures the detonator (24) to the base plug

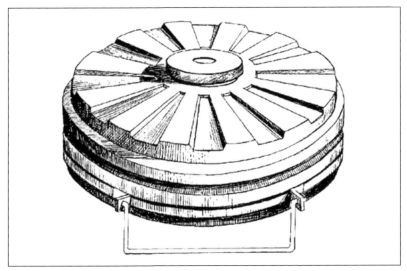

FIG. 3

(25) of the igniter body (26). The igniter mechanism consists of a spring-loaded striker (27) held by a shear pin (28). Pressure on the pressure plate, acting on the head of the striker, causes the shearing of the pin (28) and the release of the striker. This fires the cap (29) which in turn fires the detonator (24).

Before attempting to lift the mine, a search should be made around the edge of the mine and in the base to discover the presence of additional igniters. If any are found they should be neutralized and the attached wires cut. The screwed plug (18), when unscrewed, can be removed, thus revealing the igniter below. When the igniter is lifted out, the mine is disarmed since the detonator is attached to the igniter. The additional igniters should then be unscrewed, and the detonators below them removed.

c. Tellermine No. 3

A third type of German Tellermine has been reported (see figure 3). This mine is 12 1/2 inches in diameter, with a maximum height of 3 3/8 inches. It has a total weight of 21 pounds and is painted a matte gray. It has the following markings:

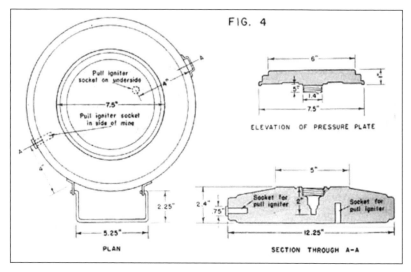

FIG. 4

Pull igniter socket on underside

Pull igniter socket in side of mine

7.5"

PLAN

5.25"

2.25"

ELEVATION OF PRESSURE PLATE

6"

7.5"

.5"

1.4"

SECTION THROUGH A-A

Socket for pull igniter

Socket for pull igniter

5"

12.25"

2.4"

.75"

- On the top, in white paint: T. Mi S31 Tvii. 2.42
- On the top, in black paint: S 88 12 42A.
- Stamped on the top: WO 42

In this model, the pressure plate extends over the entire top of the mine, and is fluted or grooved, probably to prevent sand being blown off when the mine is buried. In the center of the pressure plate is a threaded socket, closed by a screwed plug with, a milled head. This socket will take the standard brass igniter assembly as used with Tellermine No. 1 but the mine can also be used with igniter assembly of Tellermine No. 2, the igniter being inserted through the central socket and the screwed plug then replaced. Both types of igniters have been found in the field. The subsidiary igniter sockets are located on the bottom and side of the mine in the same places as in Tellermine No. 1.

d. Tellermine No. 4

The details of a fourth type of German Tellermine have recently become available. Tellermine No. 4 is circular in plan (see figure 4) with a diameter of 12.25 inches and over-all height of 3.4 inches. The base is flat and the cover slightly dome-shaped. The total weight of the mine is approximately 18 pounds. The mine is painted field gray, and the pressure plate black.

Stencilled on the top of the mine in white is: "T. - Mi. - Pilz 43/T. - Mi. - Z42 13A"

There are two screwed holes for additional igniters, one in the side of the mine 4 inches from the carrying handle, and the other in the base, offset from the center—as in Tellermine No. 2. It has been reported that this mine has also been found with the holes for additional igniters located in the side of the mine opposite the handle and in the base between the handle and the center—as in Teller mines Nos. 1 and 3.

The pressure plate is a flat metal plate 7 1/2 inches in diameter, which screws complete into the central socket over the normal Tellermine No. 2 igniter. Neither the pressure plate nor the body of the mine is fluted.

The mine functions when pressure on the pressure plate causes the latter to descend and shear the igniter shear pin, thus releasing the spring-loaded striker.

To neutralize this mine the sides and bottom of the mine should first be examined. If additional igniters are found, they should be neutralized. The pressure plate should then be unscrewed and the igniter removed.

e. Comparison

The pressure plates on Tellermines No. 1 and No. 3 extend over the entire top of the mines, but the pressure plates on Tellermines No. 2 and No. 4 cover only the center portion of the mine. Accordingly a tank might pass over the edge or rim of Tellermines No. 2 and No. 4 without detonating the mines, whereas the same load passing over the edge or rim of Tellermines No. 1 and No. 3 would detonate the mine. It is possible for a spread-out load of fairly low intensity covering the whole top of Tellermines No. 1 and No. 3 to detonate them, while a more heavy, concentrated load is necessary to detonate Tellermines No. 2 and No. 4.

The pressure plates on Tellermines No. 2 and No. 3 are fluted

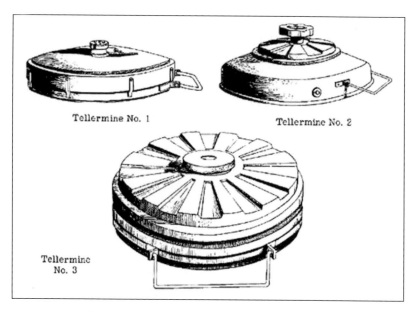

Tellermine No. 1

Tellermine No. 2

Tellermine No. 3

or grooved, but the pressure plates on Tellermines No. 1 and No. 4 are smooth.

In Tellermine No. 4, by adopting a simpler form of pressure plate and utilizing the simple igniter found in Tellermines No. 2 and No. 3, the considerable production difficulties, which were entailed in the manufacture of Tellermine No. 1, particularly its T. Mi. Z35 igniter, have now been largely overcome.

GERMAN "TANK HUNTING" TACTICS

From Tactical and Technical Trends,
No. 29, July 15, 1943.

The following information on the employment of magnetic mines by German infantry antitank squads has come from a credible German source. Six men are assigned as an antitank team, generally for night operations in positions offering possible avenues of tank approach. The team is deployed in the form of a U at intervals of approximately 50 yards, adapting itself to the terrain for observation and field of fire.

All men are armed with machine pistols and antitank, magnetic hollow-charges. The team leader, No. 4, carries a pyrotechnic pistol. In addition, four Tellermines are carried for placing in the probable path of the tank and are controlled by a 50-yard length of wire by which they can be pulled under the approaching tank.

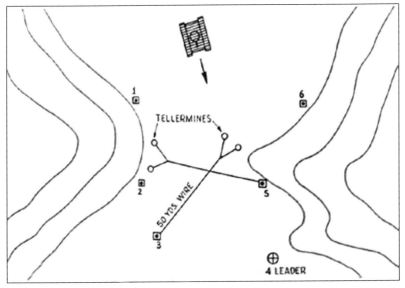

When a tank comes on, the team leader fires a pyrotechnic charge directly at the turret of the tank and momentarily blinds the crew. At the same time Nos. 3 and 5 pull Tellermines into its path, and No. 2 rushes forward to place the magnetic charge on the side armor plate of the tank. Meanwhile, No. 4 covers the turret-hatch to prevent the escape of the crew; Nos. 1 and 6 cover the ground behind the tank for possible infantry accompanying it. Each man is interchangeable with the others of the team and his duties are determined by the terrain.

A GERMAN ANTITANK MEASURE

From Tactical and Technical Trends,
No. 31, August 12, 1943.

A report from a British source states that in the North African campaign, the German tanks and antitank guns, after they had hit and immobilized enemy armored vehicles, continued to fire at them until they were either blown apart or were burning.

TACTICS OF GERMAN ANTITANK ARTILLERY

From Tactical and Technical Trends,
No. 32, August 26, 1943.

The following summary from British sources gives some recent information on the German antitank tactics. It includes notes on the theory of this type of fighting and on actual experiences from battle areas.

a. Antiaircraft Artillery in Antitank Role

A german artillery general writing in a newspaper article, stated that the AA artillery has long outgrown its original role. It has, indeed, still to undertake the AA protection of the forward positions and lines of communication, but these duties are carried out, as it were, on the side. Elements of AA artillery are now placed in the main line of resistance, and kept in a mobile condition. Their chief purpose is antitank defense, which they carry out by allowing the tanks to close to very short ranges. The first round should be, and often is, a direct hit on a vital spot. Furthermore, units of AA artillery may be also used as field artillery. They are placed in the field artillery area from 2,000 to 4,000 yards behind the main line of resistance, have their own OP's and perform all the normal artillery tasks.

b. Simultaneous Use of Various Calibers in AT Defense

Two papers, apparently from the German tank school, dealing with antitank tactics on the Russian front, state that 37-mm AT guns, although adequate against most Russian tanks, must be used in conjunction with 50-mm and, where possible, with 88-mm guns. AT guns should be concentrated in centers of resistance.

The papers also stress that long fields of fire are often a

disadvantage; the ideal field of fire is that of the effective (not the maximum) range of the gun. Enfiladed positions, and positions on reverse slopes are becoming more important. Dummy positions are very important in making the heavy Russian tanks waste the small issue of ammunition carried. Mines in front of the guns are useful in view of the Russian habit of making small raids at night in tanks equipped with blinding headlights or searchlights.

At night always, and by day usually, a 37-mm AT gun with hollow-charge ammunition should be kept ready for action. Camouflage must be good, and fire held till the last moment, as more than one shot is scarcely ever possible.

c. Layout of Gun Positions

A British antitank regiment has supplied some interesting notes on the layout of the enemy antitank defenses in Africa.

(1) In general, gun pits appeared to be sited with no attempt at defilade; there were few instances of guns being in mutual support of each other. The 88-mm pits and the majority of pits for the 47-mm Italian guns were in the main line of resistance. There did not appear to be much depth in the layout of either of these types. The 20-mm Breda guns were in the rearward emplacements, thus giving a certain degree of depth to the position.

(2) Two 88-mm pits were examined, both well up in the main line of resistance—one was in fact sited in an opening in the foremost double-apron fence, about 50 yards in front of which was a low trip-wire. The gun was sited to fire straight to the front down a valley, to a distance of about 3,000 yards. Both AP and HE shells were found in this pit. The second pit was similar, but did not have as long a field of fire.

(3) Only two 47-mm pits were found in which there had been any attempt to get defilade from the front. None of these is considered to have been well-sited. In the majority of cases, pits were found (often in pairs about 50 yards apart) in the

main line of resistance and sited to fire straight out over the wire, which was, on an average, 40 to 50 yards distant.

d. Company Tactics in Africa

(1) Tactics in a Static Role

The German antitank company commander is given a sector to defend, which he sub-allots to platoon commanders. Each gun in a platoon is then given a definite sector within which the No. 1 of the gun has complete freedom of action. Fire was not controlled by the company commander. Rapid changes of position were possible only with the aid of tractors which were kept as near as possible to the gun positions. There were no drag-ropes on the guns and manhandling beyond a few yards was exhausting.

(2) Formation When Advancing

The company formation was for the three platoons to advance in line of platoons. Two guns in each platoon were forward, about 200 yards apart, and the third gun in support 200 yards behind, and equidistant between the forward guns. The distance varied, however, to suit the ground. When cooperating with, and protecting the flanks of tanks, a liaison officer was assigned to the tank unit by the antitank battalion.

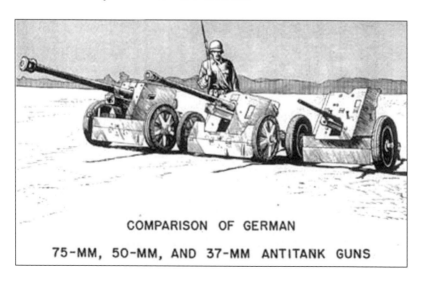

COMPARISON OF GERMAN

75-MM, 50-MM, AND 37-MM ANTITANK GUNS

GERMAN CONVERSION OF FRENCH 75S INTO ANTITANK GUNS

From Tactical and Technical Trends, No. 34, September 23, 1943.

Conversion by the Germans of French M-1897 75s to make them suitable for use as antitank guns is described in a translation of an article in a recent issue of a Fighting French publication. The writer of the article comments that the captured French artillery, as converted, may serve as hard-hitting, mobile weapons in antiinvasion operations. It is stated that Germany probably has "a good few thousand" of the French 75s which were captured in Poland and France prior to 1941.

Principal features of the conversion of the French 75s are described as follows:

The barrel seems to have undergone only two external modifications:

(1) The addition of a muzzle brake. This brake, which is of the Bofors type, seems to be exceptionally large. If it is compared with a brake of the same type mounted on high-powered Bofors 75, it can be estimated that it absorbs at least 33 1/3 per cent of the recoil.

In all probability the initial velocity is increased. (The regulation initial velocity of the 75, model 97, firing model 10 armor-piercing, shell was about 1,800 f/s. Before the war it was possible to obtain an initial velocity of about 2,000 f/s with the model 36 Gabaud shell weighing 13.23 pounds. It can be assumed that the initial velocity of the converted gun will be slightly over 2,000 f/s.

(2) The addition of a light box on the upper part of the barrel

a little in front of the supports of the clinometer. Its function is not known but it may be the device for establishing the lead on a moving target.

It does not seem that the position of the trunnions has been changed. The disequilibrium created by the addition of the muzzle brake has been compensated for by the addition of a single equilibrator, low-powered and vertical, acting on the right trunnion of the oscillating cylinder.

The Germans have mounted the gun on a 5-cm Pak 38 carriage known as Pak 97/38 or on a 7.5-cm Pak 40 carriage, when it is known as Pak 97/40.

Although a field piece cannot be judged solely by appearance, the conversion described above seems to be particularly good. The only improvements that have not been effected are the automatic opening of the breech and the firing of the piece by the gunner.

NEW GERMAN 88-MM AT GUN

From Tactical and Technical Trends,
No. 38, November 18, 1943.

A photograph has been obtained of what is presumably a new AT gun. Although it is not possible to give accurate details of the weapon from the illustration, the barrel bears some superficial resemblance to that of the 8.8 cm Flak 41 (see Tactical and Technical Trends No. 29, p. 5) while the carriage shows considerable similarity with the mount which is interchangeable between the 105-mm gun (10.5-cm K-18) and the 150-mm medium field howitzer (15-cm s F.H.), both standard equipment for the German infantry division. It seems probable, therefore, that the weapon is the Pak 43, which is believed to be the barrel and recoil assembly of the 8.8-cm Flak 41 on a field mounting for use principally as an antitank gun, with no AA role, and with which the name "Hornet" has been connected.

The accompanying sketch has been made on the assumption that the barrel of the 8.8-cm Flak 41 fitted with a muzzle brake is, in fact, mounted on a modified carriage for the 105-mm gun and the 150-mm howitzer, with the addition of a low shield. It will be noted that the recoil cylinder and recuperator are now mounted below the barrel in accordance with the German antitank gun practice. In the sketch, the trails are shown as fitted with small ice spades and mount the large spade in the carrying position.

NEW GERMAN 88-MM ANTITANK GUN

THE 75/55-MM AT GUN, PAK 41

From Tactical and Technical Trends,
No. 40, December 16, 1943.

An account of a new and powerful tapered-bore 75-mm AT gun made by the Rheinmetall factory, the 75/55-mm (2.95-in/2.17-in) Pak 41, has recently become available through Allied sources. The gun has a curious bore; the rear part is cylindrical and rifled; the central part, tapered and unrifled, and the muzzle section — 27.6 inches — cylindrical and unrifled. The weight of the powder charge fired is 95 per cent of the weight of the projectile. With an estimated velocity of approximately 4,000 f/s, and a penetration of 5.94 inches of homogeneous armor at 1,000 yards, the gun is most formidable.

a. General

The 75-mm Pak 41, one of the latest German antitank guns to be brought into service, is the third* of the Gerlich or tapered-bore weapons introduced. In issue No. 7, p. 3 of Tactical and Technical Trends, reference is made to the use of this principle in the 42-mm Pak 41. A 75-mm tank gun, the 7.5-cm Kw.K 41,

THE 75/55- MM AT GUN

is also known to exist, and it is very probable that this weapon too is of the tapered-bore variety. The caliber of the 7.5-cm Pak 41 at the breech is 75 millimeters (2.95 in), while at the muzzle it is reduced to 55 millimeters (2.17 in). The reinforced breech is of the vertical wedge type, and is semiautomatic. There is a muzzle brake. The weapon is very long, low and sturdy in appearance. The carriage which has a split trail, is unusual but extremely simple. The cradle is attached to the shield, which forms the basis of the carriage, by what is, in effect, a spherical universal joint. The cradle itself is cylindrical, and covers the whole of the rear half of the barrel. The gun is sighted up to 1,500 meters (1,635 yards), and the sight has four scales for use according to the actual muzzle velocity of the gun, which drops considerably owing to wear. The life of the barrel is provisionally estimated as 500 to 600 rounds.

The shield is composed of 2 1/4-inch plates bolted together with the barrel installed in a ball mount.

The elevating mechanism, of the sector type, is on the right-hand side of the cradle. The traversing mechanism is of the screw type and is on the left. There is no equilibrator. The buffer is hydraulic, and the recuperator is spring type. The wheels are metal with solid rubber tires. Traction is motorized. The axle is under-slung with torsion-bar suspension, which is automatically cut out when the trails are opened. Pneumatic brakes, controlled by the driver of the tractor, are fitted.

b. Gun Data
- Estimated muzzle velocity:4,123
- Length of barrel (approx): 170 in
- Weight in action: 1.4 tons (British long)
- Elevation: -10° to +18°
- Traverse: 60°
- Height of axis of bore at 0° elevation: 34.6 in
- Length of recoil (approx): 27.6 in

c. Ammunition

Fixed ammunition is used with an AP tracer projectile of Gerlich design (see accompanying sketch). The AP round is known as 7.5-cm Pzgr. Patr. 41 Pak 41 (Armor-piercing shell Model 41 for Pak 41).

The projectile consists of the outer case (1), the tungsten carbide core (2), the screw-head (3), the ballistic cap (4), and the

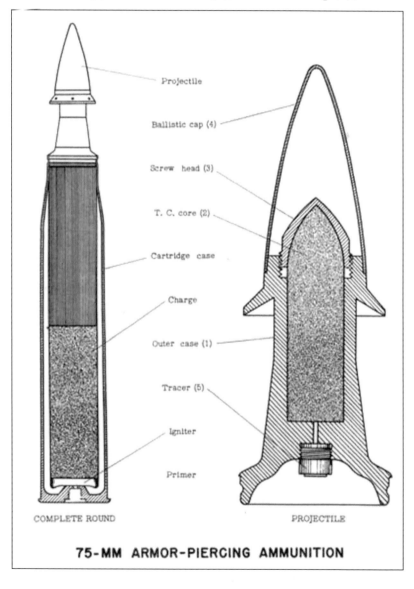

75-MM ARMOR-PIERCING AMMUNITION

tracer (5). The outer case has a forward and a rear skirt. Only the forward skirt is perforated. The screw-head is made of mild steel.

The propellant charge is diglycol tubular powder, while the igniter is of pyroxylin porous powder.

There is also an HE round (7.5-cm Sprgr. Patr) (HE shell Model 41 for Pak 41) as in the cases of the 2.8-mm s.Pz.B (antitank gun) 41 and the 4.2-cm Pak 41, but no details of this ammunition are known.

The following are brief specifications of the AP ammunition:

- Total weight of round: 16.65 lb
- Total length of round: 29.8 in
- Weight of projectile: 5.68 lb
- Weight of tungsten carbide core: 2.01 lb
- Diameter of core: 1.16 in
- Weight of propellant charge: 5.4 lb

d. Penetration

The following figures for penetration of homogeneous armor by this weapon firing the AP projectile have been estimated:

Range	Thickness of armor in inches	
(yards)	Normal	30°
500	(6.67 in)	(5.75 in)
1,000	(5.94 in)	(5.12 in)
1,500	(5.28 in)	(4.49 in)
2,000	(4.63 in)	(3.94 in)

*The other two are: the 2.8-cm (1.10 in) heavy antitank rifle and the 4.2-cm (1.65 in) light antitank gun.

NOTES ON GERMAN ANTITANK TACTICS

From the Intelligence Bulletin, February 1944.

1. ANTITANK METHODS IN RUSSIA

The following observations represent an authoritative Soviet view of German antitank methods:

The German antitank defenses open up while our [Soviet] armor is moving toward the front line or when it has reached its line of departure. First, German bombers and artillery go into action to halt our attack, or at least to delay it.

The German artillery (GHQ units, divisional units, and in rare instances regimental guns) lays down a barrage about 2 miles inside our lines, and tries to smash our armor. Each German battery is assigned a frontage of about 100 to 150 yards, which it must cover. When our tanks are within 200 to 300 yards of the antitank obstacles on our side of the German main defensive area, the German guns transfer their fire to the accompanying Soviet infantry.

When our tanks are within 600 to 1,000 yards of the German main defensive area, single antitank guns (chiefly regimental) are brought into action. The main antitank strength opens up only when the range has been reduced still further, and is between 300 and 150 yards. The guns which constitute the main strength are sited principally for enfilade fire from well-camouflaged positions.

The Germans site most of their antitank weapons to the rear of the forward edge of their main defensive area. Only single guns are sited along the forward edge; their mission is to engage individual tanks. As soon as an attack has been repelled, these guns change position. Antitank reserves are placed in areas most vulnerable to tank attack, especially at boundaries between units. Infantry antitank reserves consist of a platoon of antitank guns and several tank-hunting detachments, and are sometimes reinforced by infantry, field guns, and tanks.

Positions are planned for all-around defense. Two or three alternate positions are prepared for each antitank gun. Roving guns are used extensively, especially in the less vital areas. Assault guns and self-propelled antitank guns are used, not only as a mobile antitank reserve, but also as fixed weapons dug-in near the forward edge of the main defensive zone.

The main antitank weapon strength is concentrated against the flanks and rear of the attacking tanks. Gun positions are protected by antitank mines and by tank-hunting detachments. Very often, too, the Germans mine the ruts made by retreating tanks, in the hope that Soviet tanks will use them as a guide.

As the Soviet tanks reach the German main defensive line, tank-hunting detachments go into action. At this stage smoke may be used, but only if the antitank guns have ceased firing, inasmuch as smoke hinders accurate laying. When the tanks reach the German gun positions, the field guns fire over open sights.

2. ENGAGING TANKS AT CLOSE RANGE

The following order was issued by the general officer commanding the Fifteenth Panzer Division during the last days of the Tunisia fighting:

The general officer commanding the Army Group Africa desires that, as a rule, the antitank artillery engage hostile armored vehicles at ranges of not more than 800 yards, and that special attention be paid to close-range engagement of tanks by tank-hunting detachments. I repeat my instruction that training in close-range engagement of tanks with all weapons shall be stressed. Every man in this division who knocks out a tank in close combat will receive the Assault Badge and, in addition, a special leave.

3. AN ANTITANK COMPANY LAYOUT

The following description of a German antitank company layout was provided by a prisoner of war. Since this layout would be dictated entirely by terrain factors, it should be regarded as an instance of enemy flexibility, rather than as a typical arrangement.

Platoons were in line, with their guns echeloned. Each platoon had two guns forward, about 200 yards apart, and a third gun to the rear, equidistant from the other two. The distance to the nearest gun of the adjoining platoon was about 300 yards. On each side of the gun position, there was a light machine gun, in line with the forward antitank guns and about 30 yards from the nearest neighboring gun.

GERMAN AIRBORNE 28/20 AT GUN

From Tactical and Technical Trends, No. 45, April 1, 1944.

Prior references to the German 28-mm AT Gun (M 41) will be found in Tactical and Technical Trends No. 5 p. 14, No. 26 p. 7. The 28/20-mm AT gun Model 41, s.Pz.B.* 41, has now been produced in a lighter mounting for airborne use. The carriage of the new model is made of light tubular metal and it is equipped with small pneumatic wheels. The weight of the barrel and the cradle is the same in both models, but the total weight of the airborne version is only 260 pounds as compared with 501 pounds for the older version. Other features of interest are:

(a) A weakening at the junction of the body and trail leg (at which point there was a fracture on a mounting examined).

(b) The sleigh and cradle complete with trunnion band are

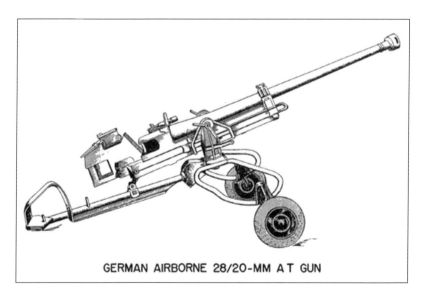

GERMAN AIRBORNE 28/20-MM A T GUN

aluminum alloy casting (probably duralumin).

(c) The gun has free elevation and traverse.

(d) To absorb the kick due to breech preponderance on recoil, an elevation shock absorber is mounted between the cradle and the saddle.

(e) The two wheels have about half the diameter of those on the heavier field mounting. They are mounted on swinging arms clamped by serrated disks. In the firing position the wheels are swung upwards, leaving the gun to rest on the tubular framework on the forward end.

*schweres Panzerbüchse - heavy antitank rifle

GERMAN ANTITANK WEAPONS

From the Intelligence Bulletin, November 1944.

German antitank weapons are divided into several classes. The main class comprises guns built specifically for antitank missions and falls into three groups—guns of conventional German design, guns built with tapered-bore tubes, and captured antitank weapons.

The orthodox German guns in the first group are designed to achieve armor penetration at maximum ranges by using relatively heavy projectiles with high velocities. The first such gun was the 37-mm Rheinmetall (the 3.7-cm Pak). This was too limited in power at the time of the Battle of France (1940), and was superseded by the 50-mm 5-cm Pak 38. This 50-mm weapon is gradually being replaced, in turn, by the 75-mm 7.5-cm Pak 40, which is the standard German antitank gun of today. Since the Pak 40 is capable of penetrating 4.43 inches of armor at 500 yards, it is considered an adequate weapon. These three guns all have similar basic features: split tubular trails, a low silhouette, and a large shield. All have been kept as light as possible to increase tactical mobility. The 50-mm and the 75-mm guns employ muzzle brakes to reduce recoil and thus permit lighter carriages. In 1944 another gun, the 88-mm 8.8-cm Pak 43/41, was added to this group. Although this gun is extremely powerful (it penetrates 4.4 inches of armor at 2,500 yards), its great weight on its split-trail, two-wheeled carriage somewhat reduces its mobility. Another version of this gun—the 8.8-cm Pak 43—mounts the same tube, but on a carriage like that of the well-known 88-mm antiaircraft guns of the Flak 18 and 36 types.

The guns in the tapered-bore group are intended to have greater mobility than conventional guns capable of achieving identical armor penetration. Tapered-bore guns seek to achieve

The tapered-bore 28/20-mm gun, s.Pz.B. 41.

The airborne 28/20-mm antitank gun.

penetration at short ranges, using light projectiles fired at very high muzzle velocities. Tungsten, which is becoming increasingly difficult for the Germans to obtain, is necessary in the manufacture of projectiles for these guns; also, the performance of the guns in combat has been a disappointment to the Germans. All three of the tapered-bore guns bear the same date of standardization—1941. First to be introduced was the very light 28/20-mm gun 2.8-cm s.Pz.B. 41. So light that it can easily be manhandled by one gunner, the 28/20 has been used by mountain troops, who can break it up into loads and climb with it, and also has been used in an airborne version. It has been issued extensively to armored and motorized infantry as a rifle company antitank weapon. The next larger tapered-bore gun, the 42/28-mm 4.2-cm Pak 41, is mounted on a modified 3.7-cm Pak carriage; this weapon also has been used by mountain troops. The largest is the 75/55-mm 7.5-cm Pak 41. The 75/55 has a most unusual carriage. There is no axle; instead, the wheels are secured to the thick shield, with the gun trunnioning on the shield as well. This gun has not been issued in large quantities.

The group of captured antitank weapons includes a number of types that the German Army had seized in the course of its conquests. Most of these guns had been designed and built before 1940. The Germans have used them as stop-gap weapons, substituting them for the better matériel that German factories have not been able to produce in sufficient quantity. For example, extensive use is made of the French Model 1937 47-mm gun (4.7-Pak 181 (f)), which has an effective range of only

The tapered-bore 42/28-mm 4.2-cm Pak (right) resembles the 3.7.cm Pak (left).

The 75/55-mm tapered bore 7.5-cm Pak 41.

The French Model 1937 47-mm Gun.

Two non-German guns that the German Army uses in an antitank role are shown at the left and right. At the left is the French 75 fitted with a muzzle brake and mounted on the Pak 38 carriage. At the right is the Russian Model 1936 field gun rebuilt as the 7.62-cm Pak 36 (r). The gun in the center is the gun with which the Russians intended to replace the Model 1936; it is known as the 76.2-mm Model 1939 field gun. The Germans have fitted it with a muzzle brake, and although they class it as a field gun, they also use it in an antitank role.

550 yards. However, there are two really useful and efficient weapons that the Germans have put to considerable use. One is the Soviet 76.2-mm Model 1936 field gun, which the Red Army designed with an eye to using it for antitank and even antiaircraft purposes. The Germans have found this high-velocity gun valuable, and have modified it by adding a double shield and, sometimes, a muzzle brake. Although it is an alternate weapon with the 75-mm Pak 40 and the 88-mm antitank guns in the German Army, the Soviets have found it too heavy and badly balanced, and have issued what they consider superior antitank and field guns to replace it. Another foreign gun favored by the German is the famous 75-mm Schneider field gun, Model 1897.

Many of these have been captured from various European countries, especially from France. The Germans have modified the 75-mm Schneider by fitting it with a large muzzle brake and by putting the gun on their own 50-mm antitank gun carriage. They call the result the 7.5-cm Pak 97/38. Since the French 75 lacks muzzle velocity, it cannot be regarded as a satisfactory modern antitank gun.

A second and highly important class of antitank weapons consists of antiaircraft guns employed in an antitank role. The high velocity of antiaircraft guns makes them suitable for antitank missions, and, since 1940, German designers have paid special attention to the possibility that any German antiaircraft gun may be used as a dual-purpose weapon. The smaller guns—the 20-mm 2-cm Flak 30 and 38, and the 37-mm 3.7-cm Flak 18 and 36—are now of little value in an antitank role because of their lack of power. They remain effective against lightly armored vehicles, and against the vision slits, ports, and optical apparatus of larger tanks. The newer 50-mm 5-cm Flak 41,

The 20-mm antiaircraft gun, 2-cm Flak 38.

The 8.8-cm Flak 36, emplaced (in Russia). When this gun is off its carriage, as shown here, it can fire against aircraft. However, the Germans fit it with a shield when they intend to use it primarily against tanks.

which resembles the 37's, is not much more effective. The 88mm guns are notorious for their effectiveness against tanks of all sizes. These guns include the Flak 18 series (that is, the Flak 18, 36, and 37) and the Flak 41. Those in the Flak 18 series have mobile cruciform carriages with four outriggers, and are capable of effective fire with heavy projectiles at great ranges. They differ in minor details only. The Flak 41 is a somewhat similar weapon, but much more powerful, having a greatly increased muzzle velocity. Introduced in 1942, it is similar to the 8.8-cm Pak 43/41 in that its great weight renders it less mobile than would seem desirable. Fitted with a large shield, it was designed with greater consideration for antitank fire than were the guns in the Flak 18 series. The latter, as a matter of fact, usually are fitted with a special carriage and shield when they are to function primarily in an antitank role. This carriage permits a limited field of forward fire from the wheels without the necessity of emplacing the gun. A Soviet gun—the 85-mm Model 1939— has been fitted with an 88-mm liner, and is now in German service as the 8.5/8.8-cm Flak 30(r). This gun bears a general

142

resemblance to those in the Flak 18 series, and gives a similar performance.

It is notable that, in the case of most of the guns mentioned, the Germans have made every effort to cut down on weight so as to gain tactical mobility. While the use of light metals and lighter carriages through employment of recoil-reducing muzzle brakes has been general, there has been a recent tendency to retain mobility but to increase muzzle velocity by reducing the gun-tube safety factor. This appears to have been done even in the case of such heavy weapons as the 88-mm Pak 43/41 and the Flak 41. The tendency has been especially noticeable in German adaptations of such captured weapons as the Soviet Model 1939 antiaircraft gun and the Soviet Model 1936 field gun, the chambers of which have been altered to take more powerful charges.

Another important class of antitank weapons is composed of the self-propelled antitank guns, or tank destroyers. These generally comprise modern antitank guns mounted on lightly

An 8.8-cm Flak 41 emplaced (in Italy).

The 88-mm tank destroyer Rhinoceros.

armored tank chassis. Typical of the best of this class are the Rhinoceros (an 88 mounted on a modified tank chassis made of Pz.Kpfw. III and Pz.Kpfw. IV parts), the 75-mm 7.5-cm Pak 40 (Sf), and the 76.2-mm 7.62-cm Pak 36(r) (Sf) on the Panzerjäger II (or Marder II) chassis or the Panzerjäger 38, (or Marder III) chassis. (The terms Marder II and III refer to highly modified tank chassis of the Pz.Kpfw. II and Pz.Kpfw. 38(t), with engines moved forward so that gunners can stand on the floor of the hull. Panzerjäger is a general term referring to all highly modified chassis for German tank destroyers.) Such changes give the vehicles a lower silhouette. They represent an advance from the period 1941-42, when the Germans quickly mounted any sort of antitank weapon on any sort of chassis. Since many of the latter types of self-propelled guns are in use today, it may be said that there are as many types of German self-propelled antitank guns as there are possible combinations of guns and chassis.

One of the latest and most powerful tank destroyers is the Jagdpanther, or Panzerjäger Panther. This weapon is an 88-mm gun of late design on a Panther tank chassis, suitably modified. The gun is so well armored that there is actually hard to distinguish the Jagdpanther from an assault gun.

German assault guns now must be listed as a class of available antitank weapons, although their primary mission is direct infantry support. The most common type of assault gun is the long 75-mm gun with muzzle brake, mounted on a Pz.Kpfw.

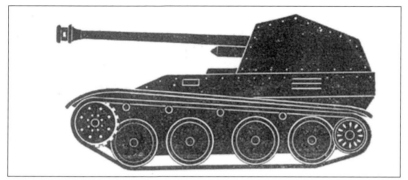

A 75-mm tank destroyer on a modified chassis—7.5-cm Pak 40 (Sf.) auf Pz. Jäg. 38 (Marder III).

A 75-mm tank destroyer on a modified chassis—7.5-cm Pak 40 (Sf.) auf Pz. Jäg. II (Marder II).

76-mm tank destroyer on an unmodified chassis—7.62-cm Pak 36 (r) auf Pz. Kpfw. 38 (t).

III chassis. This type is known as the 7.5-cm Sturmgeschütz 40. A big assault gun formerly called the "Ferdinand," but now known as the "Elephant," mounts an 88. It is thought that production of this heavy 70-ton vehicle may have been

The 88-mm tank destroyer Jagdpanther.

discontinued. German assault guns of the types mentioned have guns mounted in low armored boxes, instead of in turrets. Fire is only to the front, with very limited traverse. Armor is weak on the rear and top.

German development of the hollow-charge shell, which began as early as 1938, has permitted employment of all low-velocity infantry howitzers and field artillery in emergency antitank roles. The principle of the hollow charge is well known. Low-velocity weapons merely have to throw their hollow-charge projectiles against an armor surface. On striking the armor, the light streamlined cap of the shell is crushed. The explosive then exerts a concentrated force against a small area of the armor. The concentrated blast which results is intended to effect a penetration of the tank armor.

Hollow-charge shells have been furnished for standard infantry guns and artillery of German divisions of all types — in particular, the 75-mm and 150-mm infantry howitzers, the 105-mm and 150-mm field howitzers, and the 105-mm guns.

Since many antitank guns of obsolete models still are in service, the Germans have introduced the stick bomb, another development of the hollow charge, in an effort to make the most of such equipment. Stick bombs consist of very large charges mounted on a spigot. The spigot is inserted in the gun muzzle,

146

A side view of the widely used 75-mm assault gun, 7.5-cm Stu. G. 40.

A top view of the 7.5-cm Stu. G. 40. This is a slightly earlier model than the one shown in the preceding photograph. Removable anti-bazooka/antitank grenade plates are in place.

and the whole is propelled by firing a special blank round. Stick bombs are furnished for the 3.7-cm Pak, 15-cm s. I.G. 33, and the French Model 1937 47-mm antitank gun. Such bombs have short range and limited accuracy. The French 47, for instance, fires its stick bomb at ranges of from 200 to 275 yards only.

A most important class of antitank weapons was almost

The Ofenrohr, with the projectile used in it and in the Püppchen.

completely neglected until Germany invaded the Soviets. Only then, apparently, did the German High Command become seriously interested in the effectiveness of close-combat antitank weapons and techniques. The Germans were in such a hurry to introduce this type of warfare that the first German manuals on the subject hardly bothered to change the Soviet drawings that they copied. As a result, German soldiers studying antitank close combat were treated to illustrations which showed Soviet troops successfully demolishing Pz.Kpfw. I's with all varieties of close-combat weapons.

Prior to the Russian campaign, the Germans had issued a company antitank weapon—the 7.9-mm antitank rifle. But after the Russian campaign had got under way, the Germans began to convert this weapon into a grenade launcher which could fire hollow-charge antitank grenades.

Readers of the Intelligence Bulletin already are familiar with the simpler devices used in close antitank combat—Molotov cocktails, bottles of phosphorus, sliding and hand-thrown mines, magnetic hollow charges, sticky bombs, and weapons of a similar nature. Readers also are familiar with such weapons as the antitank hollow-charge grenade which can be launched from the standard rifle, and with the signal pistol fitted to fire hollow charges. However, the non-recoil weapons of the bazooka type—a most important group—have not yet been discussed.

Of this group the first weapon to be adopted was a frank copy of the bazooka. The larger German version is called the 8.8-cm Raketenpanzerbüchse 43, or Ofenrohr (stovepipe) for short. Sometimes it is called the Panzerschreck—(tank terror). The

Ofenrohr fires an 88-mm hollow-charge projectile weighing 7 pounds. The maximum range is about 165 yards. The Ofenrohr is clumsier than the bazooka, and is reputed to be less accurate.

The Püppchen ("Dolly"), a carriage-mounted rocket launcher with breechblock also fires the 88-mm rocket. Although the Püppchen has wheels, the gun can be fired from little sleighs to achieve a very low silhouette. While the Püppchen, has a range of 770 yards, is very lightly built, and is likely to smash up when towed by motor vehicles.

The great majority of the non-recoil weapons are devices known as Panzerfaust. There are three of these—the little Panzerfaust klein 30 (formerly the Faustpatrone I), the Panzerfaust 30 (formerly the Faustpatrone II), and the Panzerfaust 60. The little Panzerfaust is called Gretchen for short, while the 30 is known simply as Panzerfäuste. The tubes are similar, and have a sight and firing mechanism. They are 1 3/4 inches in diameter and 2 feet, 7 1/2 inches long. The projectiles are very large hollow charges. The charge for the Gretchen weighs 3 pounds, 4 ounces; that for the Panzerfaust weighs 6 pounds 14 ounces. Each is mounted on a wooden tail

The Püppchen.

The Panzerfaust 30, with sight raised and projectile shown separately. The projectile vanes are extended.

A U. S. soldier demonstrates the Panzerfaust klein 30.

rod fitted with spring-steel vanes. These vanes wrap around the rod when the rod is inserted in the muzzle of the launching tube, and spring out to guide the projectile after firing. The tubes are expendable, and contain the propelling charge fired by percussion. The range is very limited, and is indicated by the designation (30 means 30 meters range, or 33 yards; 60, 66 yards). The operator must take cover after discharging a projectile. Also, he must wear a helmet as protection against a rain of fragments and debris, keep his eyes closed, and keep the front edge of his helmet against the ground. The jet of flame to the rear is fatal up to 10 feet; the operator must take this into account when firing, and make sure that no walls or other obstacles will block the jet. The tubes are held under the right arm. The left hand supports the front of the tube, while the right hand is free to pull out the safety pin, cock the striker, and press the release button. Sighting is effected by aligning the top of the sight and the top edge of the projectile. To date, all the Panzerfäuste have proved dangerous to the user. It is believed that every effort will be made to improve them—especially with regard to increasing the range. Armor penetration is good; the Germans claim as much as 7.9 inches for the Panzerfaust 30. It is estimated that actual penetration is around 6 inches.

Since Allied airpower has curtailed the mobility of German antitank guns, the Germans have been compelled to place great stress on the Ofenrohr and the Faustpatrone. Large quantities of these have been issued. The Ofenrohr is chiefly a regimental antitank company weapon, but the Faustpatronne is furnished on a generous scale to each rifle company. Reports from the field indicate that the Faustpatrone has been especially well liked by German soldiers.

An even more recent development is the Panzerwurfmine. This is a hand-thrown hollow charge; it is similar in size and shape to the Faustpatrone projectiles, except that its vanes are made of cloth.

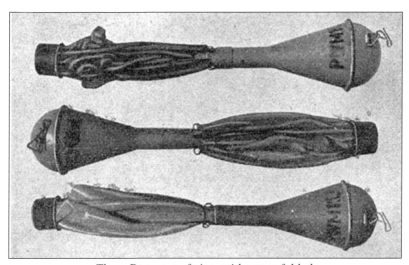

Three Panzerwurfmine, with vanes folded.

Glossary of German Terms

- Elefant (Elephant) — an 88-mm gun mounted on the Panzerjäger Tiger P (a highly modified Tiger tank chassis). This was formerly known as the Ferdinand.
- (f) — a French weapon officially adopted by the German forces. The letter follows the weapon designation.
- Faustpatrone — obsolete name for a Panzerfaust.
- Flak (Flugabwehrkanone) — antiaircraft, or antiaircraft gun.
- Gr.B. (Granatbüchse) — a special rifle for launching antitank grenades.
- Jagdpanther — an 88-mm antitank gun mounted on the Panzerjäger Panther (a highly modified Panther tank chassis).
- Marder (Marten) — name of a bird, used to designate three types of tank destroyer (Panzerjäger) chassis:
- Marten I — the Panzerjäger Lr.S. chassis, which is a highly modified French Lorraine tractor chassis.
- Marten II — the Panzerjäger II chassis, which is a highly modified Pz.Kpfw. II chassis.
- Marten III — the Panzerjäger 38 chassis, which is a highly modified Pz.Kpfw. 38(t) chassis.
- These chassis when designated Marten mount either the 75-mm Pak 40 or the 76.2-mm Pak 36 (r).
- Nashorn (Rhinoceros) — an 88-mm antitank gun mounted on the Panzerjäger III/IV, and formerly known as the Hornisse (Hornet). (The Panzerjäger III/IV is a highly modified chassis made from parts of the Pz.Kpfw. III and IV.)
- Pak (Panzerabwehrkanone) — antitank, or antitank gun. (Panzerjägerkanone is the new word for antitank guns, but the abbreviation still is Pak.)
- Panzerfaust — a recoilless, one-man antitank grenade launcher. At one time Panzerfaust referred only to one

Demonstration throwing of the Panzerwurfmine.

model of launcher.

- Pz.B. (Panzerbüchse) — antitank rifle; if preceded by the letter "s", a heavy anti-tank rifle.
- Pz.Jäg (Panzerjäger) — (1) Antitank and tank destroyer (new term).
- (2) A chassis of some vehicle highly modified in order to mount an anti-tank gun.
- Pz.Kpfw. (formerly Pz.Kw.) (Panzerkampfwagen) — tank.
- (r) — a Soviet (Russian) weapon officially adopted by the German forces. The letter follows the weapon designation.
- R.Pz.B. (Raketen-Paazerbüchse) — a rocket launcher of the bazooka type.
- s.I.G. (Schweres Infanteriegeschütz) — a heavy infantry cannon.
- Stu.G. (Sturmgeschütz) — an assault gun (refers to complete unit of gun and carriage).
- (t) — a Czechoslovakian weapon officially adopted by the German forces. The letter follows the weapon designation.

HOW TO THROW THE PANZERWURFMINE

From the Intelligence Bulletin, March 1945.

An antitank hand grenade has been developed by the Germans for use by infantry troops in close combat against tanks. Known as the Panzerwurfmine, this weapon is capable of penetrating 3 inches of homogeneous armor plate, and may be thrown as easily as an ordinary stick grenade.

The Panzerwurfmine, which weighs about 3 pounds, consists of a cone-shaped body with a hemispherical end, and with the stick handle attached to the other, or point, end of the cone. The most novel feature of this weapon is a set of four collapsible cloth vanes which are folded against the handle. When the grenade is thrown, the vanes spring open and presumably guide the projectile head-on to the target.

The conical head of the grenade is filled with a hollow charge designed to direct the force of explosion in one direction—against the armor plate of the target. Built to detonate on impact, the grenade fuze is located in the butt end of the hollow wooden handle, which is filled with an explosive booster charge. The fuze—a striker pin held back from a primer cap by a weak spring—detonates when the force of impact overcomes the

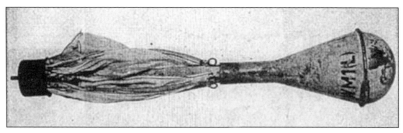

The Panzerwurfmine is a hollow charge, antitank hand grenade. When in unarmed condition, the cloth vanes, which tend to guide the projectile head-on to the target, are held folded against the grenade handle.

(1) The soldier who uses this grenade must grasp the handle in such a way that the collapsed vanes will be held closed against the handle when the retaining cover is removed. Then, and only then, can the cover be removed by straightening the metal tongue and slipping the cover free of the handle and fuze assembly.

(2) Once the cover is removed, the grenade is ready for throwing. The weapon is thrown in the same manner as the ordinary stick grenade. When the grenade leaves the thrower's hand, the steel ribs on the handle will be released from tension and snap out to extend the sail-like vanes.

(3) When released in this fashion, the rib tied to the metal clip pulls the clip clear of the fuze assembly, releasing the safety-pin tape. The drag of air on the tape pulls the safety pin free, and the striker pin is armed to detonate when the grenade strikes the target.

weight of the spring and throws the striker against the cap. A safety pin which fits into the top of the fuze assembly keeps the fuze in an unarmed condition until the grenade is thrown. The fuze assembly is housed in a thin metal cylinder fitted over the end of the wooden handle.

The grenade is armed in flight when the loosely seated safety pin is pulled free by the drag of air on a short cloth tape, one end of which is fastened to the free end of the pin.

Near the cone end of the handle, four spring steel ribs are secured in grooves. When extended, umbrella-fashion, these ribs are the framework for the cloth vanes. When the vanes are collapsed, the ribs are held under tension flat against the handle, and are secured in position by a metal cap which fits over the end of the fuze assembly and the free ends of the folded ribs. This cap is held in place by a metal tongue on the fuze assembly. The tongue passes through a slit in the cover.

During transport the tape attached to the safety pin is secured under a horseshoe-shaped metal clip which snaps around the outside of the fuze assembly, thus holding the safety pin in place. A short piece of string is tied from the clip to the end of one of the folded steel ribs.

Although the Panzerwurfmine may seem easy to use, it requires a degree of caution upon the part of the thrower, who must be sure that the vanes remain closed—thus keeping the grenade unarmed—until the weapon leaves his hand.

GENERAL ERHARD RAUS
REPORT

Hitler as well as the invited listeners apparently were well aware that I was now about to touch upon the encirclement and annihilation of X SS Panzer Corps and elements of Corps "Tettau," and would give the reasons for these developments. (See report of my second discussion with Himmler.)

Since this disaster can only be traced to his orders, which were forwarded by Himmler and were contrary to all proposals made by my army, he, by this interruption of the report, prevented me from speaking freely on the subject and offer his own orders as evidence. This assumption is substantiated by the fact that the part of my report up to this point dealing with the tactical developments of the Pomeranian battle must have been just as familiar to him from the army reports as that portion which would clearly show the dramatic effects of his personal orders.

After this unexpected change in my report, I described a number of small combat events which well illustrated the behavior of troops and commanders. They seemed the most appropriate as a reply to Hider's question, "How the commanders and troops behaved in battle."

Examples of Valor

1. After the breakthrough on 22 February 1945 south of Stegers, enemy tanks suddenly appeared at the outskirts of Baldenburg. The antitank barriers on both ends of town, which extended over a considerable distance, were kept open for the normal through traffic. Suddenly, the guard at the barrier at the southern exit of the town saw a Russian tank approaching at full speed. He quickly attempted to place one of the heavy wooden horizontal bars into position. He did not succeed, however, and the leading enemy tank drove through, firing at the roadblock, and pushed

into the city. A second and a third T-34 followed closely behind and also attempted to pass through the barrier. However, at the last moment, the alerted guards (three men) still managed to get the crossbar in place in spite of tank fire. Nevertheless, the leading tank still tried to get into the town and consequently attempted to quickly ram the obstacles, but in so doing was set on fire by a Panzerfaust. A rifleman firing a second shot hit the next tank and put it out of action as well. In the meantime, another soldier from the construction engineer unit also destroyed with a Panzerfaust the lead tank, which had advanced into the town. When the tank unit became aware of the fate of its lead tanks, it stopped, widely scattered, in a small patch of woods close by and halted its advance for the day. As a result, a few 50- year-old soldiers, through their calm, courageous action, were able to bring the initial penetration of fifteen tanks to a halt, and thus enabled the weak local holding force to defend, unaided, the village until the following day. The successful Panzerfaust men had seen enemy tanks for the first time in their lives and had put them out of action. For their valor, they were awarded the Iron Cross, Second Class.

2. The tank unit referred to above, after having been substantially reinforced near Baldenburg, broke through the switch position. The very weak holding force of the Pomeranian Division maintained its position against all the attacks of the enemy's motorized units, and thus only the tanks were able to open a very narrow gap along the front, which was closed a number of times by the defending forces. As a result, the momentum of the tank attack aiming at Bublitz had been crippled. That was one of the main reasons for lack of aggressiveness displayed by the unit as it reached the gates of the city, where it remained for two days. The other reason was the unit's insecure position in the woods, where it was continually surprised by mobile tank destroyers. On one day alone, it lost sixteen tanks, and on the following day twelve more were knocked out by tank destroyers which went

after them in the woods. In this manner, the tank assault against Koeslin was delayed. Maps showing the future plans of the tank unit were found in one of the wrecked tanks.

3. In order to widen the gap and protect the south flank of the enemy tank unit which had penetrated at Baldenburg, an enemy infantry unit supported by three T-34s turned off toward the southwest, took the village of Bisohofthum, and advanced toward Kasimirshof. This town was held by a small detachment of approximately twenty construction engineers under the command of a line NCO who, having been badly wounded, had temporarily been placed in charge of highway construction workers. Besides rifles, the detachment had only one machine gun, and the NCO was armed with two Panzerfausts. When he noticed the enemy approaching, he deliberately and very calmly issued the order: "Everyone take cover in the foxholes here on the outskirts of the village and permit the leading three tanks to roll by without firing on them. I will take care of these. Fire on the infantry following them at a range of 500 meters and prevent their entrance into the village. I shall station myself behind this house on the main street of the village and wait for the tanks." A few minutes later, one by one and carefully maintaining intervals, the tanks rolled into the village. The NCO knocked out the last tank with one Panzerfaust, whereupon the second tank turned toward the group of houses, firing in movement toward the spot where he presumed resistance came from. But, using bushes as cover, the NCO had already crept up close to the tank, and from only a short distance had knocked out this tank as well with the last Panzerfaust. When the lead tank saw the other two go up in flames, he pulled out of this sinister town by a side street and started on his way back. In so doing, he pulled the enemy infantry pinned down by the defensive fire of the detachment along with him. Immediately, the courageous NCO, together with his men, took up the pursuit, and during the counterattack also recaptured the village which had been lost earlier. The NCO

was again badly wounded during this action. So much for the description by his battalion commander, to whom I spoke personally at the main aid station in the presence of wounded participants of that action.

4. On 25 February, air force reported another unit of 22 tanks in a place 25 kilometers southeast of Koeslin. A detachment of antitank fighters of about 60 men, which had immediately started out in that direction, stalked through the woods near the village. At night, a strong reconnaissance patrol was dispatched to the village under cover of darkness and was to locate the tanks. During their reconnaissance, the patrol noticed a light in a house and Russian officers were observed as they sat at their evening meal. The window was ripped open in one quick movement, and at the same moment a hand grenade was thrown into the room. At this signal, the antitank fighters rushed into the village, firing rapidly as they came, and thus threw the surprised tank unit into utter turmoil. After brief fighting, a number of tanks were knocked out and set ablaze. In the ensuing confusion, the remaining tanks quickly evacuated the village, which remained in our possession two days longer. Shortly thereafter, I was able to contact the courageous antitank fighters myself over the telephone from Koeslin.

5. For three days, the reconnaissance battalion of the 10th SS Panzer Division "Frundsberg," having been moved up recently, had brought strong enemy tank columns to a stop with their assault guns at Regenswalde and Plathe and thus rendered the westward evacuation of long columns of vehicles and carts from Kolberg possible. Subsequently, in action at Greifenberg, the battalion prevented a turning maneuver and the further advance of enemy tank units aiming at Stettiner Haff by offering stubborn resistance until it became completely encircled. Through the exertion of its last ounce of strength, the battalion blasted its way out of the tank encirclement and broke through to its own lines.

6. During early March 1945, a tank unit suddenly appeared

at one end of the autobahn running from Stettin to the east, with the obvious intention of advancing rapidly toward Stettin on the best possible road. This was prevented by setting up a barrier at that point, which was guarded by a weak covering force. The small detachment of valiant soldiers was surrounded and fired upon from all sides by enemy tanks. By using Panzerfausts and an antitank gun which was knocked out later, the detachment prevented the tanks from entering the autobahn. In this effort, the detachment dwindled to only a few men. Finally, after two or three hours of this unbalanced struggle, the enemy abandoned his plan when some of our own Tiger tanks approached. Six enemy tanks which had been set ablaze were the price the enemy had to pay in this effort. The autobahn remained in our hands.

7. In order to prevent the establishment of a bridgehead east of Altdamm, tank units attempted to strike from the north via Gollnow into the rear of III SS Panzer Corps, which was engaged in bitter fighting along both sides of the Stargard—Stettin highway and railroad line. This was prevented by a reinforced armored infantry regiment located in the area of Gollnow after fighting bitterly for the town and railway station. For more than a day the struggle surged back and forth. Numerous enemy tanks were destroyed, but our own forces also suffered heavy losses. Enemy tanks, initially focusing their efforts on the railroad station, drove into the area of our own artillery, which fought to the last round but was finally subdued. Two batteries were destroyed in the course of this heroic struggle. These sacrifices, however, saved the corps from a much worse fate.

8. Encircled by the enemy, elements of Corps "Tettau" were fighting in the rear of the enemy near Regenswalde, and gready harassed his operations. Recently, the army had reestablished radio contact with this force and had ordered it to turn northward and attempt to reach the coast west of Kolberg, so that it might fight its way forward along the coast to the Divenow bridgehead. This unit reached the coast yesterday. Instructions as well as

orders were transmitted to this force by means of a liaison plane [Fieseler Storch], which had to detour far out over the sea. The unit should arrive in Divenow in a few days.

9. Yesterday (7 March), an enemy unit with 34 tanks, in an attempt to reach the large bridge, broke through the Divenow bridgehead, which was being defended by young naval personnel. The navy troops, well-trained in the use of the Panzerfausts and under the command of Army's antitank officer, had neither antitank guns nor artillery, but were solely equipped with rifles and a few machine guns, besides many types of Panzerfausts. Armed with only these weapons, they took up a fierce pursuit and knocked out 33 of the 34 tanks which had broken through. One enemy tank which had already reached the bridge across a tributary was blown up, together with the bridge.

10. And, just before coming in, my chief of staff reported to me that an enemy tank attack was again carried out today against the same bridgehead held by the navy troops. The enemy, however, never reached our positions because the young navy troops, greatly impressed by the previous day's victory, did not wait for the attack of the 36 advancing enemy tanks echeloned in width and depth. On the contrary, the navy troops, disposed along a broad front, jumped off and in disorganized fashion attacked the rapidly firing tank unit from all sides, and, regardless of their own heavy losses, forged ahead toward the tanks until they were within effective Panzerfaust range. In a short time, all 36 tanks were knocked out. Their death-defying courage in relying on the Panzerfaust brought about a complete victory. This unsurpassed heroism will someday go down in the annals of German history.

Conclusion

"My Fuhrer, the report should clearly indicate that the commanders of both large and small units, as well as the troops and the individual soldiers, have done everything in their power to withstand the vastly superior enemy forces. They lacked neither ability, willingness, nor courage, but they did not possess superhuman strength. They all fought bravely and tenaciously, even when the situation was hopeless, since no one wanted to be guilty for the loss of German territory. In spite of being outnumbered from 6 to 20 times in manpower and equipment, the command and troops endured the utmost hardships in trying to avert a complete collapse of the front. "It can be explained only in this way—that in spite of all the existing needs, the front has been firmly reestablished in bridgeheads east of the Oder, even to the extent of being able to launch a successful counterattack at the southern wing, where yesterday 86 enemy tanks were knocked out, and ground suitable for further stabilization of a defensive front was gained.

"As a peculiarity of the Pomeranian battle, I can report that of the 580 enemy tanks which have been knocked out up to this time, 380, or two-thirds, were destroyed by the Panzerfaust— that is, by the courage of the individual soldier. Never before has an army achieved so much success with the Panzerfaust.

"Therefore, I can only express my complete appreciation to my commanders and all the troops of the army for the great courage and self-denial shown in the unbalanced struggle for Pomerania."

Final Observation

The Fuhrer and the others present were obviously impressed by my remarks, but did not utter a word. I was dismissed by a trembling nod of Hitler's head. My successor arrived the next day at my headquarters in Stettin with a Fuhrer order, and, in accordance, I had to turn over command of the army to him and was transferred to the officers' reserve pool. That was the end of my 40-year tour of service. A few days later Reichsfuhrer SS Himmler was also relieved of his command as Commanding General Army Group "Weichsel."

GERMAN ANTITANK ROCKET LAUNCHER

From Tactical and Technical Trends, No. 46, May 1, 1944.

A new German antitank rocket launcher (Raketenpanzerbüchse 43) has been examined. In appearance it is very similar to the American "Bazooka" but larger. The German nickname is Ofenrohr or "stovepipe".

a. Description

(1) Launcher

This consists of a plain pressed steel tube with three indented guides. Below the tube is the cocking handle and trigger mechanism protected by a square steel guard. To the rear of the trigger is the induction coil which is connected by a lead to the socket at the rear of the tube. Between the coil and the socket is the shoulder rest. On the left of the tube is an offset foresight and an adjustable rearsight. The distance between sights is approximately 18 inches. At the rear of the tube is a protector and spring catch.

(2) Projectile

This consists of a hollow-charge, HE-filled head with a nose fuze containing a safety pin which is removed before firing. A body containing the rocket propellant and a tail with a contact plug is set in a small crescent-shaped wooden block. The propellant consists of a single stick of "diglykol."

b. Action

The crew of the weapon consists of two men - a firer and a loader. The loader inserts the projectile into the rear of the tube far enough to allow the spring catch to snap over the tail end.

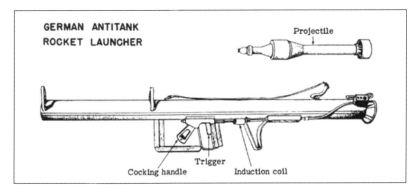

GERMAN ANTITANK ROCKET LAUNCHER

Projectile

Trigger

Cocking handle

Induction coil

This catch retains the projectile in position.

The plug on the projectile is fitted into the socket at the end of the tube. After cocking, by pulling the handle to the rear, the weapon is ready for firing.

When the trigger is depressed, the soft iron rod is driven a short distance through the coil thereby inducing a current to pass through the lead to the plug and igniting the propellant. Owing to the softness of the iron core it can only be used seven times. After that the residual magnetism is too low to produce sufficient current.

The firer should wear a gas mask, a face mask, steel helmet and protective clothing to avoid burns from the escaping propellant gases.

c. Data

- Length of tube: 5 ft 3 in
- Diameter of tube: 3.46 in
- Thickness of tube: .06 in
- Weight of tube: 20.5 lb
- Weight of projectile: 7.3 lb
- MV of projectile: 345 f/s
- Range of projectile (approx): 164 yds
- Penetration of armor (German source): 7.87 in

The smallest firing unit is generally made up of a six-man team, equipped with three launchers, and they are usually stationed in strong-point formation so they can fire in any direction.

NEW HOLLOW-CHARGE ANTITANK GRENADE FOR CLOSE COMBAT

From Tactical and Technical Trends,
No. 51, October 1944.

The new German Faustpatrone, a recoilless antitank hollow-charge grenade with expendable launcher, designed as a basic close-combat antitank weapon, is the latest German development in close-combat antitank matériel. The tables of issue give 36 to each rifle company, and a total of 2,000 to the infantry division. The Ofenrohr (German "bazooka," also called Panzerschreck) remains the basic close-combat weapon of the regimental antitank company.

Close-combat antitank methods and matériel are strongly emphasized by the German Army as a result of experience on the Eastern front. Their dependence on these methods is now increased by United Nations supremacy in the air and superiority in fire power, which interdict effective employment. of German antitank guns, forcing them to be sited with more consideration for cover than would normally be the case. This air and fire power hamper fulfillment of antitank-gun missions and cause heavy losses in crews and matériel. Antitank close-combat matériel then becomes still more important to the Germans, not only for defense, but to maintain the morale of German troops in the face of Allied armor.

During 1943 and 1944 the Germans still showed ingenuity and resourcefulness in adapting their tactics and matériel to changing conditions, in learning from their opponents, and in making the best of limitations. Prompt adoption of a German version of the U. S. "bazooka" (the Ofenrohr) and the subsequent development of the two models of Faustpatronen are examples.

Antitank close combat, which has been discussed before both in this publication and in the Intelligence Bulletin, lends itself to many variations in organization, equipment, and method, according to local conditions, the matériel available, and the ingenuity and aggressiveness of the troops.

As an example of the need for adaptability, the Germans used smoke grenades successfully on the Eastern front to blind opposing tanks, but the Soviets, after first making the error of stopping, learned to drive right through the smoke, preferring the risk of what might be on the other side of the cloud to the certainty of attack if they came to a halt.

The Ofenrohr (also called Panzerschreck, and described in the May 1944 issue of Tactical and Technical Trends) is a basic weapon of the regimental antitank company, in which two platoons may each have 18 Ofenrohr.

SECTION OF THREE LAUNCHERS

The smallest tactical unit for employment of this weapon is the section of three launchers. These are usually sited close behind the infantry positions, on which they depend for close protection. If the terrain is open, the launcher subsections may be sited in an irregular line so that there is not more than 130 yards between weapon pits. Thus, even if one crew is knocked out, there will be no gap in the defense, since the area can still be covered from the two nearest pits.

A section is sited well forward of the infantry positions only when it is absolutely certain that tanks will be encountered, since in forward positions the section is too vulnerable to patrols or unexpected attacks. In this case the pits are carefully camouflaged.

According to German doctrine, if tanks come within range of two launchers at once, both should engage simultaneously, partly to make certain of a kill, and partly to insure that each subsection does not leave the target to the other.

The weapon pit has three parts, a firing trench, a loading trench, and a shelter trench. The section consists normally of two men, No. 1 firing the launcher and No. 2 serving as loader. Sometimes a second-in-command and a runner may be added, the runner carrying ammunition from the rear, and both replacing casualties and engaging crews from damaged tanks. The section may also be equipped with either model of the Faustpatrone and the usual variety of close-combat antitank equipment, such as magnetic hollow-charges, smoke grenades, Molotov cocktails, sliding mines, pole charges, plus sub-machine guns, pistols, rifles, and hand grenades.

The 88-mm rocket launcher (Püppchen), with breechblock and wheels, described in the August 1944 issue of this publication, should not be confused with the Ofenrohr, even though both fire the same ammunition. Püppchen is not a close-combat weapon, it has a range reported at 700 yards as against 200 yards for the Ofenrohr, and it sometimes replaces some of the antitank guns in the division anti-tank battalion.

The antitank rifle in its original form is entirely obsolete, though an attempt was made to increase its effectiveness by modifying it permanently to launch an antitank hollow-charge grenade. The race between armor and armament has brought about the use of increasingly larger projectiles and an increase in muzzle velocity in some weapons to increase penetration. But the development of the hollow-charge principle has enabled the effective use of low-velocity weapons against tanks. With the hollow-charge principle the penetration is independent of the velocity, because the effect depends on concentrating the explosive force in a jet.

TABLES OF ISSUE

The German tables of issue for close-combat antitank weapons to various units are heavy, especially in the case of the recoilless antitank grenade with launcher as far down as companies.

The Ofenrohr is issued as follows:

1. Tank-destroyer battalion with antitank guns and close-combat antitank weapons (Panzer-Zerstörer Bataillon), 216.
2. Infantry divisions, light divisions, and mountain divisions, 130, of which 22 are kept in reserve, and 18 are issued to each of 2 platoons of the regimental antitank companies.
3. Armored divisions, Panzergrenadier divisions, GHQ troops, and corps units are not equipped with this weapon.
4. Ammunition is issued at a basic rate of 10 per "bazooka," replacements being allotted as necessity requires.

The Faustpatronen are issued on a very heavy scale:

1. Infantry divisions, light divisions, and mountain divisions: To each infantry, light, mountain, and engineer company, 36; to each antitank company, 18; to each artillery battery, 12; to other units, 18 per company; total, 2,000 for the infantry division.
2. Panzergrenadier division, 1,500.
3. Armored division, 1,000.
4. GHQ units, 70 per battalion.
5. Corps units, 50 each.

The order in which units are to be equipped with these weapons is as listed above. (For example, the infantry, light, and mountain divisions, have priority over the Panzergrenadier divisions.) It should be borne in mind, however, that the present state of German supply will result in many inconsistencies in issue and in deviations from the established scale.

It appears that "bazookas" have been ordered withdrawn from rifle companies and replaced by either of the two models of the Faustpatrone.

There are two models of the Faustpatrone, the Faustpatrone 1, also called the Gretchen; and the Fauspatrone 2, also called the Panzerfaust. The literal translation of Faustpatrone is "fist cartridge."

Both are hollow-charge grenades, and easily fired by one man. The grenades and launchers are identical in operation and similar

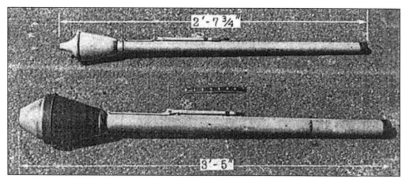

Recoilless antitank grenades, with launchers.

in design, except that the Gretchen is somewhat smaller than the Panzerfaust (see figure). Both of these weapons have a maximum range of less than 50 yards, but improved models with longer ranges may be encountered. Penetrations are claimed by the Germans of 5.5 inches (140-mm) for the Gretchen and 7.9 inches (200-mm) for the Panzerfaust, although it is estimated that the penetration of the latter is actually no more than 6.5 inches (165-mm).

The weapons consist of two main parts, a simple launching tube with a sight and firing mechanism, and a hollow-charge grenade with wooden tail and spring-steel fins. The weight (grenades only) of the Panzerfaust is 6 pounds 14 ounces; the Gretchen, 3 pounds 9 ounces.

Outstanding features of these weapons:

1. Absence of recoil, which is neutralized by the escape of part of the propellant gases to the rear — on the same principle as the Germans' airborne guns.
2. A comparatively large projectile for the weight and size of the launcher.
3. Simplicity of operation and design.
4. The low velocity of the grenade does not lessen its effectiveness, because of the hollow-charge principle.

The expendable launching tubes of thin steel, open at both ends, contain the propelling charge, which is fired by percussion. Attached to the top of the tube is a bracket which contains a bolt for cocking the firing mechanism, and at the front end a release

170

button and simple folding sight.

The grenades have thin steel heads containing the hollow charge. The filler is believed to be Cyclotol (Cyclonite and TNT). The outside of the wooden tail unit is provided with spring-steel fins. One end of each fin is so attached to the tail that it may be wrapped around the tail for loading in the launching tube.

The grenade may be launched from standing, kneeling, or prone positions. The operator must always wear a steel helmet, and immediately after firing must take cover to avoid being hit by splinters. Since a 6-foot jet of flame shoots from the rear of the tube on firing, a firing position must be so chosen that there will be no walls or other obstructions to this stream.

In firing, the tube is taken under the right arm, the left hand supporting the tube about 2 inches from the front end.

The weapon is then sighted over the top of the sight and the top edge of the grenade.

The fuse safety pin is pulled out, and the striker is cocked by pushing the lock forward until the striker is set and the release button emerges. The lock then slides back into its original position, and the release button is pressed, discharging the grenade.

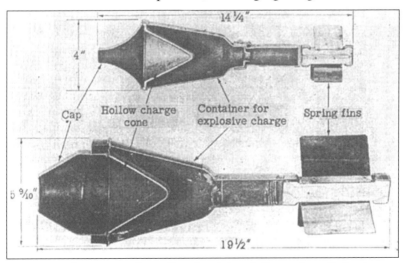

Grenade cross-sections: Gretchen (above), Panzerfaust (below).

88-MM GERMAN ANTITANK GUN USED IN FRANCE: GENERAL DATA

From Tactical and Technical Trends, No. 51, October 1944.

Detailed information is now available concerning the German 88-mm (3.46-in.) antitank gun Pak 43/41 which was first encountered by United States forces in France, although it had been employed previously against the Soviets. General data:

- Length of tube, including muzzle brake: 258.66 in.
- Length of muzzle brake: 17.35 in.
- Maximum traverse (30° R, 30° L): 60°.
- Rate of traverse: 1 turn per 34".
- Maximum elevation: 36°.
- Maximum depression: 7°.
- Height of wheels: 48 1/2 in.
- Maximum recoil: 28 in.
- Minimum recoil: 24 in.
- Length of carriage without gun: 216 in.
- Length of carriage with gun: 360 in.
- Height of carriage in traveling position: 78 in.
- Total weight of equipment: 9,660 lb.

The carriage of this equipment follows orthodox lines with trail legs hinged to a bottom carriage upon which is mounted a cradle providing lateral deflection and carrying the usual layout of traversing and elevating gears. The wheels, on cranked stub-axles, are independently sprung but there is no compensation between the wheels, and the carriage is on four-point support when firing. In general, the carriage appears as if it might be one of the earlier designs of field carriage adapted to take the Pak 43/41 gun.

The barrel is made in two sections. The front end of the rear section has an enlarged diameter which is prepared for the reception, jointing, and securing of the rear end of the front section. The correct positioning of the rifling is ensured by a key which is inserted from the outside. A locking collar, similar to that used on all German guns to lock barrel to breechring, locks the front section to the rear section, thus preventing longitudinal movement. Use of this locking collar obviates the necessity for start of thread. A gas seal is provided by inserting a steel expansion ring between the two sections of the barrel. This ring fits into recesses cut in each section.

The front section is supported by the rear section for a length of 32 inches and has two bearing surfaces, one at the front end and one at the rear end: these have a clearance of 0.004 and 0.003 inch respectively.

The lug which takes the recoil cylinder is not connected to the breech ring but is a part of a bracket welded to a band which splits into halves and is forward of the breechring. Breechring and mechanism are similar to the 75-mm Pak 40, slightly simplified. The gun is fired electrically, with two 2-volt batteries in series provided on the left side of the carriage. The muzzle brake is similar to that found on the Pak 40, Pak 36, and other guns. but in this case the rear baffle only is bushed.

The cradle is a welded design. It is attached to the carriage by a pintle at the rear and two adjustable rollers in the front. These rollers bear on a plain machined arc. Underneath the cradle a flat machined plate is attached by two bolts, and this plate in turn fits underneath the plain arc and serves as a stop to any upward movement of the cradle in firing.

The hydropneumatic recoil mechanism is on top of the gun. The pressure is 800 pounds per square inch. The buffer is housed in the cradle underneath the gun and is of orthodox design.

The elevating gear is arc-and-pinion type and is normal with the exception of two hand wheels, one on each side. The left handwheel can be used for final aiming, as it has a ratio of one and one-half turns to one of the right handwheel. The gun is fired from the left wheel. The traversing gear is normal, controlled by a handwheel to a worm on the center of the cradle, then to a worm-and-pinion onto the traversing rack on the carriage.

The trail is split and of riveted construction. It is rather short, only 10 feet 6 inches in length.

Attachment of the spades is interesting. They are forward, on top of the legs, in the traveling position and fold back over the legs for firing. The legs are locked in the traveling position by two locking devices, one of which also locks the cradle, and the other also locks the lunette in position. The lunette folds back and locks on the inside of the right leg when in the firing position.

The 88-mm Pak 43/41 may be confused with the 88-mm Pak 43 because of similar designation. While both have tubes based on the tube of the 88-mm Flak 41, the Pak 43 has a cruciform carriage not unlike that of the 88-mm Flak 18 and 36. However, the Pak 43 carriage does not permit sufficient elevation for AA fire.

Ammunition listed below is fired by the 88-mm Pak 43/41:

Type	Approximate weight of projectile	MV (f/s)
HE (with point-detonating quick and delay fuze)—88-mm Sprgr Patr 43, Kw. K. 43 m. A. Z. 23/28	20.68	2,296
HE (with combination point-detonating quick and time fuzes)—88-mm Sprgr Patr 43, Kw. K. 43 m. Dopp. Z. S/60 Fl. or Dopp. Z. S/60 V	20.68	2,296
APCBC—88-mm Pzgr Patr 39/43, Kw. K. 43 m. Bd. Z. 5127	22.44	3,280
AP40—88-mm Pzgr Patr 40/43, Kw. K. 43	16	3,775

TANK DESTRUCTION BADGE

The Tank Destruction Badge (Sonderabzeichen für das Niederkämpfen von Panzerkampfwagen durch Einzel-kämpfer) was an award given to individuals of the Wehrmacht who destroyed an enemy tank single-handedly by an hand-held weapon. Anti-tank units were not eligible for this award. It was established by Adolf Hitler on March 9, 1942 but could be awarded for actions after June 22, 1941 (Operation Barbarossa).

Notable recipients
- Günther Viezenz 21 kills
- Adolf Peichl 11 kills
- Johannes-Matthias Hönscheid 7 kills
- Michael Pössinger 5 kills
- Oskar Wolkerstorfer 4 kills
- Walter Kuhn 4 kills. He destroyed 4 Russian tanks within 20 minutes and received the Knight's Cross of the Iron Cross for that action.
- Franz Bäke 3 kills
- Ekkehard Kylling-Schmidt 3 kills
- Urbano Gómez García 2 kills
- Hans Dorr 2 kills
- Sylvester Stadler 2 kills
- Günther-Eberhardt Wisliceny 2 kills
- Karl Auer 1 kill
- Ernst-Günther Baade 1 kill
- Rudolf Demme 1 kill
- Heinz-Georg Lemm 1 kill
- Werner Mummert 1 kill
- Joachim Peiper 1 kill
- Theodor Tolsdorff 1 kill

Awarding the tank destruction badge